# Postpositivism and Educational Research

D. C. Phillips and Nicholas C. Burbules

ROWMAN & LITTLEFIELD PUBLISHERS, INC.
*Larham • Boulder • New York • Oxford*

ROWMAN & LITTLEFIELD PUBLISHERS, INC.

Published in the United States of America
by Rowman & Littlefield Publishers, Inc.
4720 Boston Way, Lanham, Maryland 20706

12 Hid's Copse Road
Cumnor Hill, Oxford OX2 9JJ, England

British Library Cataloguing in Publication Information Available

**Library of Congress Cataloging-in-Publication Data**

Phillips, D. C. (Denis Charles), 1938–
    Postpositivism and educational research / D.C. Phillips and Nicholas C. Burbules.
        p.  cm.  —  (Philosophy, theory, and educational research)
    Includes bibliographical references and index.
    ISBN 0-8476-9121-7 (alk. paper) — ISBN 0-8476-9122-5 (pbk. : alk. paper)
    1. Education—Research—Philosophy.  2. Positivism.  I. Burbules, Nicholas C.
II. Title.  III. Series.
    LB1028 .P46   2000
    370'.7'.2—dc21                                                    99-049770

♾™ The paper used in this publication meets the minimum requirements of
American National Standard for Information Sciences—Permanence of
Paper for Printed Library Materials, ANSI/NISO Z39.48–1992.
Manufactured in the United States of America.

# Postpositivism and Educational Research

## Philosophy, Theory, and Educational Research

Nicholas C. Burbules, Series Editor

Books forthcoming in this series:

# Contents

# Illustrations

# Series Preface

This book with Denis Phillips is the first in a projected series that will appear with Rowman and Littlefield Publishers: "Philosophy, Theory, and Educational Research." Contemporary educational research has been experiencing an explosion of new methodologies and approaches to inquiry. Many of these approaches have drawn from philosophical or theoretical positions that underlie their determinations of research methods, aims, and criteria of validity. Yet, the substance of these philosophical or theoretical assumptions is not always made clear to readers, and so it is difficult for them to judge those assumptions for themselves.

This series is designed to explore some of the dominant philosophical and theoretical positions influencing educational research today, in a manner that does justice to the substance of these views and shows their relevance for research aims and practices. Each volume will show how a particular set of philosophical and theoretical positions affects the methods and aims of educational research and will discuss specific examples of research that show these orientations at work. The emphasis is on lively, accessible, but theoretically sound explorations of the issues. These books are intended to be of interest not only to educational researchers, but to anyone in education wanting to understand what these various "isms" are about.

This series features a distinguished international group of scholars. It is important for the reader to know that the first author of each volume has had primary responsibility for conceptualizing and drafting the text. The Series Editor has played a very active role in selecting the topics and organization for each volume, has interacted regularly with the first author as the text has been drafted, and has had a relatively free hand in revising the text and adding or suggesting new material. This is more than the role that editors normally play, and so second authorship seemed the appropriate appellation. But the predominant voice and point of view for each volume in the series is the first author's. It could not be otherwise, since no coauthor could advocate equally all the positions, many of them mutually inconsistent, argued for in these volumes.

Nicholas C. Burbules
Series Editor

# Acknowledgments

The authors of this book have been discussing the issues addressed within it with each other for two decades. For about the same period of time we have been discussing—from a philosophical perspective—issues that arise in the design and conduct of educational research with colleagues who are active researchers, and with graduate students in our classes who were about to become active researchers. We have profited enormously from the feedback we have received from these interactions over the years, and from the insights into the "nuts and bolts" of research that these others have shared with us. Either singly or together, we also have had lively discussions bearing on the topics in this book with philosophical friends and colleagues in the international community, and we are especially appreciative of the time we have spent talking with Harvey Siegel, Deborah Kerdeman, Nel Noddings, Robert Floden, James Marshall, and Michael Peters. Denis Phillips has had the opportunity to present workshops on this material to researchers and graduate students in Australia, New Zealand, Israel, Norway, Sweden and Switzerland, where he learned much from the somewhat different views and assumptions about educational research that are held there. Our wives, Valerie and Joyce, have been pillars of support but at the same time the friendliest of critics. Finally, we wish to thank Jill Rothenberg and Dean Birkenkamp of Rowman and Littlefield, who have encouraged and shepherded this project from its initial conception.

# What Is Postpositivism?

When I find myself in the company of scientists, I feel like a shabby curate who has strayed by mistake into a drawing-room full of dukes.

W. H. Auden

Poet W. H. Auden penned these words almost four decades ago, in an age that is long gone. Physicists and other natural scientists may still be regarded with awe, but there can be little doubt that social scientists have fallen from their pedestal—if ever they occupied one! For the intervening decades have seen the rise to popularity of philosophical views that challenge the status of science as a knowledge-producing enterprise, and social scientists and educational researchers have been particularly vulnerable to these attacks. Scientists—according to these views—are no less human, and no less biased and lacking in objectivity, than anyone else; they work within frameworks that are just that: *frameworks*. And, these critics suggest, none of these frames or paradigms, considered as a whole unit, is more justified from the outside than any other. Philosopher Paul Feyerabend even argued that the modern scientific worldview is no more externally validated than medieval witchcraft, and the prophet of postmodernism, Jean-Francois Lyotard, held that we should be "incredulous" about the story that is told to justify science as a knowledge-making frame (its justificatory "meta-narrative," as he termed it). If this general line of criticism is true of physics or medicine, it certainly should be true of social science, in which the values and cultural background of the researcher seem to play a more pervasive role. Thus a key question arises: Can this line of criticism, particularly in the case of educational research, be met? The present book is dedicated, if not to restoring social scientists and educational researchers to their pedestal, then at least to raising them above the mire. They may never be members of the nobility, but perhaps they can be located in the ranks of those with a modicum of respectability!

Educational researchers constitute a community of inquirers. Doing the best they can and (at their best) ever alert to improving their efforts, they seek enlightenment or understanding on issues and problems that are of great social significance. Other things being equal, does lowering class size for students in the lower elementary grades improve their learning of math and reading? Does it have an effect on their development of a positive self-image? Does bilingual education enable "language minority" students (or at least a significant number of them) to master English while maintaining their progress in other subjects such as science, math, and history? What are the features of successful bilingual programs? Are whole language approaches to the teaching of reading more successful than the phonics approach (and if so, in what respects)? Does either of these approaches have serious, unintended side effects? What effects do single-sex schools have on the math and science attainment of female students? Do they have other effects of which policy makers (and parents and teachers) ought to be aware? Does the TV program *Sesame Street* successfully teach young viewers such things as the alphabet, counting skills, and color concepts? Is it more successful than the instruction children can get from parents who, say, read books to them regularly? Does this program have an impact on the so-called achievement gap that opens up at an early age between many children from impoverished inner-city backgrounds and those from well-off middle-class suburban homes? Do Lawrence Kohlberg's stages of moral development apply to girls as well as to the boys whom Kohlberg studied? (Do they even hold true of boys?) Are multi-ability classrooms less or more effective in promoting learning of academic content than "streamed" classrooms? (And do they have positive or negative "social" and "psychological" effects on the students?) Are individual memories of childhood abuse (sexual or other), which are "recovered" many years later, to be trusted? Society generally, and educational practitioners and policy makers in particular, want to be guided by reliable answers to these and many other questions.

Many of us may have strong opinions about some of these issues; indeed, beliefs may be *so* strongly or fervently held that it seems inappropriate to call them merely "opinions"—we are convinced that our views are *right*. It is crucial for the theme of this book, however, to recognize that beliefs can be *false beliefs*. What appears to be enlightenment can be *false enlightenment*. Understanding can be *misunderstanding*. A position that one fervently believes to be true—even to be *obviously* true—may in fact be false. Oliver Cromwell, the leader of the Roundheads in Britain (who executed King Charles I) and himself something of a fanatic, put this thought in memorable language: "My brethren, by the bowels of Christ I beseech you, bethink that you might be mistaken" (cited in Curtis and Greenslet 1962, 42). But unfortunately he apparently did not apply this moral to himself! Humorist H. L. Mencken put it a little less solemnly: "The most costly of all follies is to believe passionately in the palpably not true. It is the chief occupation of mankind" (cited in Winokur 1987, 31).

If researchers are to contribute to the improvement of education—to the improvement of educational policies and educational practices—they need to raise their sights a little higher than expressing their fervent beliefs or feelings of personal enlightenment, no matter how compelling these beliefs are felt to be. They need to aspire to something a little stronger, seeking beliefs that (1) have been generated through rigorous inquiry and (2) are likely to be true; in short, they need to seek *knowledge*. This aim is what the philosopher Karl Popper and others have called a "regulative ideal" for it is an aim that should govern or regulate our inquiries—even though we all know that knowledge is elusive and that we might sometimes end up wrongly accepting some doctrine or finding as true when it is not. The fact that we are fallible is no criticism of the validity of the ideal because even failing to find an answer, or finding that an answer we have accepted in the past is mistaken, is itself an advance in knowledge. Questing for truth and knowledge about important matters may end in failure, but to give up the quest is knowingly to settle for beliefs that will almost certainly be defective. And there is this strong incentive to keep the quest alive: if we keep trying, we will eventually discover whether or not the beliefs we have accepted *are* defective, for the quest for knowledge is to a considerable extent "self-corrective." (Do many of us doubt that present-day theories about the causal agents in infectious diseases are an advance over the theories of 50 or 150 years ago, or that many of the errors in these past views have been eliminated? Does the failure of a particular medical "discovery" or treatment, at a given point in time, invalidate the longer-term process of exploration and experimentation?)

Accepting this pursuit of knowledge does not necessitate a commitment to a claim of "absolute truth" or its attainability. Popper, for one, believed that "absolute truth" was never going to be attained by human beings, and John Dewey put it well when, in his book *Logic: The Theory of Inquiry* (1938), he suggested substituting the expression "warranted assertibility" for "truth." (The notion of a "warrant" has its home in the legal sphere, where a warrant is an authorization to take some action, e.g., to conduct a search; to obtain a warrant the investigator has to convince a judge that there is sufficient evidence to make the search *reasonable*. If the investigator needed to have "absolute" evidence in order to get a warrant, there would be no need for him or her to conduct a further search at all!) Dewey's point was that we must seek beliefs that are well warranted (in more conventional language, beliefs that are strongly enough supported to be confidently acted on), for of course false beliefs are likely to let us down when we act on them to solve the problems that face us! It serves no useful purpose for an education or social science researcher to convey his or her "understandings" of the causes of a problem (say, the failure of students in a pilot program to learn what they were expected to have learned) to a policy maker or an educational reformer or a school principal, if indeed those understandings are faulty. The crucial question, of course, is *how* researchers are to provide the necessary warrant to support the claim that their understandings can reasonably be taken to constitute knowledge rather than false belief. Dewey gave us a clue, but it is only that—his answer needs substantial fleshing out: *Authorized conviction* (i.e., well-warranted belief), he stated, comes from *"competent inquiries"* (Dewey 1966, 8–9). And he wrote:

> We know that some methods of inquiry are better than others in just the same way in which we know that some methods of surgery, farming, road-making, navigating, or what-not are better than others. It does not follow in any of these cases that the "better" methods are ideally perfect. . . . we ascertain *how and why* certain means and agencies have provided warrantably assertible conclusions, while others have not and *cannot* do so. (p. 104)

It is the purpose of this present volume to develop, at least in outline, the case that postpositivistic philosophy of science is the theoretical framework that offers the best hope for achieving Dewey's goal, which is—or should be—the goal of all members of the educational research community. For, after all, who among us wants to aspire to *unauthorized* conviction? Who wants to knowingly carry out *incompetent* inquiries? Who wants to hold *unwarranted* beliefs? Who wants to adopt methods and approaches that cannot achieve the degree of reliable belief to which we aspire as we try to improve education? And if we want to criticize particular research findings or claims as being biased, untrue, or misleading, how is that to be done in the absence of some notion of competent, reliable, evidence-based research?  ·

What, then, is postpositivism? Clearly, as the prefix "post" suggests, it is a position that arose historically after positivism and replaced it. Understanding the significance of this requires an appreciation of what positivism was and why it was (and deserved to be) replaced. "Postpositivism" is not a happy label (it is never a good idea to use a label that incorporates an older and defective viewpoint) but it does mark the fact that out of the ruins of the collapsed positivistic approach, a new (if diverse and less unified) approach has developed. It is to the elucidation of these matters that the discussion must now turn.

## THE POSITIVISTIC ACCOUNT OF SCIENCE

Recently, one of the authors of this book was in deep discussion with a friend from another university—a professor of psychology who frequently writes on methodological matters. The quotation from Auden was mentioned, and the discussion turned to why scientists have fallen from their pedestal. "Surely it has

**Figure 1.1. Foundationalist Epistemologies**

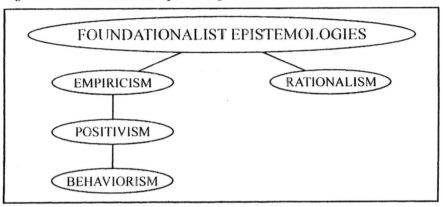

something to do with the rise of postmodernism," our intrepid coauthor suggested. "Perhaps," responded the psychologist, "but I think it is simpler than that. I believe the average person identifies science, especially in the social and educational spheres, with positivism. And because the news has gotten out that positivism is seriously flawed, the reputation of social science has suffered!"

Perhaps the psychologist was right. Certainly the image of research that has been presented in social science textbooks over the past four or more decades has been predominantly positivistic in orientation (the vast majority of texts on educational and psychological research have had—almost by mandate—a chapter addressing the nature of "scientific inquiry"). They have maintained this orientation in spite of the fact that for about the same period the philosophical flaws of this position were well known to (and widely discussed by) philosophers and others. The spread of positivism among researchers, and those who trained them, was facilitated by the influence of perhaps the best-known researcher in education-related areas for several decades, the behaviorist psychologist B. F. Skinner. His orientation was in all essential details straightforwardly positivistic. (In graduate school Skinner had read—and was influenced by—the philosophers who founded positivism.)

To philosophers, positivism (including behaviorism) is a form of *empiricism*; and empiricism in turn is one of two forms of *foundationalist philosophy*. The problems faced by positivism are merely variants of the problems that have surfaced with respect to foundationalism. The following schematic should make the relationships clear.

## Foundationalism

Until the end of the nineteenth century, all major Western philosophical theories of knowledge ("epistemologies") were foundationalist. It seemed obvious that to be labeled as "knowledge," an item had to be securely established, and it seemed equally obvious that this was to be done by showing that the item (the belief or knowledge claim) had a *secure foundation*. The great French philosopher René Descartes reflected this common orientation (and also, incidentally, recognized that many of the beliefs we hold actually are false beliefs) when he wrote in the opening lines of his famous *Meditations* (1641):

> Several years have now elapsed since I first became aware that I had accepted, even from my youth, many false opinions for true, and that consequently what I after- wards based on such principles was highly doubtful; and from that time I was con- vinced of the necessity of undertaking once in my life to rid myself of all the opin- ions I had adopted, and of *commencing anew the work of building from the foundation, if I desired to establish a firm and abiding superstructure of the sci- ences.* (Descartes 1953, 79; emphasis added)

But in order to "rebuild," he first had to identify the "foundation"; so he clos- eted himself in a small room with a fireplace and spent the winter examining his beliefs using "the light of reason," until he identified one that seemed absolutely secure and indubitable—the famous "cogito, ergo sum" (I think, therefore I am). Descartes, then, was a foundationalist and a member of its rationalist division, for he identified the foundation using his rational faculties (what [1] could not possibly be rationally doubted and [2] seemed indubitably true should be accepted *as* true).

The other branch of foundationalist epistemology—the empiricist camp—is represented well by a thinker from across the Channel, John Locke. After an evening of deep conversation with some friends that had quickly mired down, he attributed the failure to make progress in discussing important matters to the fact that our ideas are often not well founded and that the human ability to reach knowledge was not very well understood. Somewhat like Descartes, he started on an exercise of self-examination but reached a conclusion that differed from the one that the French philosopher had reached; in *An Essay Concerning the Human Understanding* (1690) he wrote:

> Let us then suppose the mind to be, as we say, white paper void of all characters, without any ideas. How comes it to be furnished? Whence comes it by that vast store which the busy and boundless fancy of man has painted on it with an almost end- less variety? Whence has it all the *materials* of reason and knowledge? To this I answer, in one word, from EXPERIENCE. *In that all our knowledge is founded; and from that it ultimately derives itself.* (Locke 1959, 26; last emphasis added)

To the empiricist, the secure foundation of knowledge is experience, which of course comes via the human senses of sight, hearing, touch, and so on. (Descartes had rejected sensory experiences as the secure foundation for knowledge because such experiences could be mistaken or illusory.)

For complex historical and cultural reasons, the primary philosophical home of empiricism for several centuries was the English-speaking world, and the primary home of rationalism was the Continent of Europe (although, as we shall see, there are important exceptions to this generalization). Despite their clear difference of opinion about the nature of the "secure foundation" for knowledge, however, they were both obviously foundationalist epistemologies. Empiricists did not deny that human rationality played some role in knowledge construction (see Phillips 1998); Locke (to stay with him as a key historical figure) certainly emphasized that the mind can manipulate and combine ideas. But the point was that the basic ideas (the units, or "simple ideas," as he called them) all came from experience. We cannot imagine the color blue, for example, if we have never experienced it (although we can be familiar with the word "blue" from reading or hearing it); but after we have a stock of simple ideas, we can combine and contrast them and build up complex ideas. Similarly, the rationalists do not deny that experience plays a role in knowledge construction, but it is subsidiary to the power of reason. As we shall see shortly, in the twentieth century there has been a recognition that although both reason and experience are important, *neither is foundational in the sense of being the secure basis upon which knowledge is built.* Much of contemporary epistemology is *nonfoundationalist.*

## Empiricism and Positivism

We need to return to the development of empiricism as an approach to epistemology, for positivism is best regarded as a "fundamentalist" version of this. Essentially there were two somewhat different points embedded in the important passage from Locke quoted above, which were teased out over the years: (1) our ideas *originate* in experience (we can trace the genealogy, as it were, of any set of complex ideas back to simple ideas that originated in sense experience), and (2) our ideas or knowledge claims have to be *justified or warranted* in terms of experience (observational data or measurements, for example). The second of these points is particularly significant; to make a claim for which no evidence (in particular, no observational evidence) is available, is (in the eyes of an empiricist) to speculate. And no matter how enticing this speculation may be, we can only accept such a claim as knowledge after the relevant warranting observations or measurements have been made. Thus, the claim that there is life elsewhere in the universe is merely a *claim* and is not knowledge until warranting observations have been made, and likewise the claim that girls undergo a different pattern of moral development than boys.

Consider another example: Suppose that while "channel-surfing" one night you find yourself watching a war movie. Suddenly it occurs to you that there might be a relationship between the number of battle movies that are made in any given period and the suicide rate in society. The more you reflect on this, the more convinced you become—war movies foster a certain callousness or at least casualness toward violent death and injury, and it seems likely to you (to your "light of reason") that this might render suicidal individuals more likely to commit this desperate act. Your hypothesis—"there is a positive correlation between the number of war movies and the suicide rate"—is *not* knowledge but is simply a hypothesis. No matter how much it appeals to the light of reason, it is an empirical/factual claim that can only be accepted as knowledge after the relevant warranting evidence has been examined (in this case, the data would be something like the numbers of war movies made per year over a longish period, say, from the late 1940s to the 1980s, with the suicide rates for those same years). It turns out that there *is* a relationship, but it is inverse—the more war movies that were made and released, in general the lower the suicide rate!

This example also illustrates several other points. In the first place, the example is phrased in terms of a correlation between war movies and suicide, but normally what interests us more is whether there is a causal relationship—whether the increased number of war movies *caused* the decrease in the suicide rate. Although the finding about the correlation mentioned above might be accurate and trustworthy, it certainly does not give one any grounds for thinking that there is a causal relationship—too many other factors were at work in society during those decades (access to television sharply increased and so the frequency of reruns of war movies on television needs to be considered; the popularity of other violent types of movies and television programs grew; and there were many sociocultural, religious, and economic changes in society that may well have affected both what kinds of movies were made and attitudes toward suicide). Second, the example illustrates that not only must empirical evidence be available but it must also be *accepted* by the appropriate research community as actually warranting the claim in question. (Actually, the point is stronger than the way it was just expressed: just as a pitch in baseball is not a strike until the umpire "calls" it, so tables of numbers or readings from instruments or records of observations or whatever are not *evidence* until the scientific community agrees to count them as such.) Most researchers would not accept the correlational data as evidence warranting belief in a causal relationship; some would regard the information about rates of production of war movies as quite irrelevant (as not being "data" at all, so far as suicide rates are concerned). Of course, these too can become matters of dispute within the relevant research community.

To return to the development of positivism, nineteenth-century philosopher Auguste Comte (who did not fit the generalization about empiricists made earlier, for he was French) seems to accepted both of the aspects of empiricism foreshadowed in Locke's work, and he argued strongly that the method of science (the "positive" method) was *the* method of arriving at knowledge. Scientific knowledge, he said, "gives up the search after the origin and hidden causes of the universe and a knowledge of the final causes of phenomena" (Comte 1970, 2) and instead focuses on observations and what can be learned by strict reasoning about observed phenomena. His work was the origin of positivism. (For further discussion, see Phillips 1992, chap. 7; Phillips 1994.)

But what if no observational evidence or data could conceivably be collected? (What if our claim was about the interior of black holes or about the human soul or about unconscious mental events that are not accessible to scientific data-gathering techniques?) A small group of philosophers, physical scientists, social scientists, and mathematicians working in and around Vienna in the 1920s and 1930s (another exception to our generalization about the Continent being inhospitable toward empiricism)—a group that became known as the *logical positivists*—took an extremely hard line on this matter, asserting that speculation about such things was nonscientific as well as *nonsensical*. They devised a criterion of meaning whereby it was literally *meaningless* to make statements about things that could not be verified in terms of possible sense experience—a criterion that renders all theological issues, for example, and Freud's theories, as strictly meaningless. They labeled such meaningless discourse "metaphysics," much to the chagrin of many other philosophers!

The work of the logical positivists became known in the English-speaking world through the writings of A. J. Ayer and others, and it was the source of B. F. Skinner's view that psychology should restrict itself to the study of behavior, for only behavior is observable. He attacked the view that there were "inner" and "psychic" causes of behavior:

A common practice is to explain behavior in terms of an inner agent which lacks physical dimensions and is called "mental" or "psychic." . . . The inner man is regarded as driving the body very much as the man at the steering wheel drives a car. The inner man wills an action, the outer executes it. The inner loses his appetite, the outer stops eating. . . . It is not the layman alone who resorts to these practices, for many reputable psychologists use a similar dualistic system of explanation. . . . Direct observation of the mind comparable with the observation of the nervous system has not proved feasible. (Skinner 1953, 29)

All such "mental events," and the "inner person" who harbors them, are strictly inferential, and Skinner labels them as "fictional" (Skinner 1953, 30); if "no dimensions are assigned" which "would make direct observation possible," such things cannot "serve as an explanation" and can play no role "in a science of behavior" (Skinner 1953, 33). In a later book he took up again his critique of the "inner man" or "homunculus" or "the possessing demon" (which he also called the inner "autonomous man"):

His abolition has long been overdue. Autonomous man is a device used to explain what we cannot explain in any other way. He has been constructed from our ignorance, and as our understanding increases, the very stuff of which he is composed vanishes. Science does not dehumanize man, it de-homunculizes him. . . . Only by dispossessing him can we turn to the real causes of human behavior. *Only then can we turn from the inferred to the observed, from the miraculous to the natural, from the inaccessible to the manipulable.* (Skinner 1972, 200–201; emphasis added)

In these books Skinner stopped just short of claiming that references to such inferred inner entities or events are meaningless, but clearly he was close to holding this logical positivist view.

Another example of the influence of positivism in education-related research fields is the wide acceptance of the need for *operational definitions* of concepts that are being investigated (such things as "intelligence," "creativity," "ability," or "empathy"). Operational definitions were first brought to prominence by physicist Percy Bridgman, a Nobel laureate, but they never caught on in the physical sciences to the extent that they became popular in psychological and educational research. (Perhaps physicists realized how much their field depended on entities that were "inferential" and not directly observable, such as quarks, black holes, and cosmological "super strings," to use contemporary examples.) Bridgman's idea was simple enough: A concept is meaningless unless the researcher can specify how it is to be measured or assessed (or how disputes about it are to be settled), and this specification has to be phrased in terms of the precise operations or procedures that are to be used to make the relevant measurements. Furthermore, if there are several different sets of operations that can be used, it can be doubted whether the same concept is involved. If a concept is defined in terms of a specific set of (measuring) operations, then if the operations are different it follows that the concepts are different (even if the same word is used in both cases to label the concepts). Bridgman made use of the simple example of length: We could define this in terms of the operations involved in using a measuring rod (laying the top end of the rod precisely alongside the top end of the object whose length is to be determined, then marking off the position of the bottom end of the measuring rod, then moving the top end of the rod down to this point and counting "one unit," etc.); but we could also measure the length in terms of the number of wavelengths of a beam of monochromatic light, and so forth. It becomes an empirical matter to be determined by experiment (and perhaps by the application of theory), whether these various methods generate the same value and whether they could be said to both measure the same "length."

The example of operational definitions illustrates that the legacy of logical positivism is a "mixed bag" instead of being entirely negative. On one hand, operationalism seems too narrow; for example, it certainly seems rash to say that it is *meaningless* to argue that Wolfgang Amadeus Mozart was more creative than Paul McCartney, simply because we might not be able to specify how to measure this (it might be a pointless or frustrating argument to have, but would it literally be "meaningless"?). On the other hand, it seems important for researchers, in most if not all cases, to be able to specify how they propose to measure or collect data bearing on some hypothesis that embodies a vague or poorly defined concept. Logical positivists were enamored of precision, which they saw as a key to the advancement of our knowledge, and if this was a failing when taken to dogmatic extremes, overall it was not too bad a failing to have! The following passage from the logical positivist Hans Reichenbach nicely embodies this spirit and also clearly displays the central tenets of this branch of empiricism:

> Now consider a scientist trained to use his words in such a way that every sentence has a meaning. His statements are so phrased that he is always able to prove their truth. He does not mind if long chains of thought are involved in the proof; he is not afraid of abstract reasoning. But he demands that somehow the abstract thought be connected with what his eyes see and his ears hear and his fingers feel. (Reichenbach 1953, 4)

As we shall see in a later section of this chapter, Reichenbach and his colleagues underestimated the difficulty of "proving the truth" of scientific statements, but the emphasis on clarity and the grounding of our beliefs on observations still stand as ideals we ought not to dismiss too lightly.

Another commentator's words can stand as a final summary:

> The logical positivists contributed a great deal toward the understanding of the nature of philosophical questions, and in their approach to philosophy they set an example from which many have still to learn. They brought to philosophy an interest in cooperation. . . . They adopted high standards of rigor. . . . And they tried to formulate methods of inquiry that would lead to commonly accepted results. (Ashby 1964, 508)

### Mistaken Accounts of Positivism

It is clear that positivists—those following in the tradition of Comte as well as those of logical positivist persuasion—all prize the methods of scientific inquiry as being *the* way of attaining knowledge. (This was clear enough in the passages quoted from Skinner, for example.) But a vital issue arises in consequence: Just what account is to be given of those methods? It is, as we shall see, a viable criticism of the positivists that they had much too narrow a view of the nature of science, and there are, of course, other problems with their general position. Despite the avenues that exist for valid criticism, it is common nevertheless to find that several mistaken charges are brought against them; labeling a person or position as "positivist" has become a favorite term of abuse in the educational research community, but it is a form of abuse that has itself become much abused!

In the first place, there is an obvious logical blunder: just because a point is made or a distinction is drawn by a positivist, it does not follow that this is a *positivist* point! Individuals of other persuasions might well be able to make the same point or draw the same distinction (for the same or for different reasons). Consider the following analogy. Biologist Stephen Jay Gould and certain fundamentalist Christian groups share some doubts about evolution as an explanatory theory, but it would be a mistake to consider them allies of one another! An example of this blunder involves the distinction that has been drawn between the so-called context of discovery and the context of justification, which was probably first recorded in the early work of logical positivist Hans Reichenbach. Others (including a vehement nonpositivist, Karl Popper) also make use of it, yet the distinction is sometimes regarded as being the hallmark of a positivist. In brief, the context of discovery is the context in which discoveries in science are first made, and the context of justification is the context in which these discoveries are justified or warranted as indeed being valid discoveries. Popper uses the distinction in large part to make the point that there is, in his view, no logic of discovery, that is, there is no set of algorithms or procedures by which one can reliably make scientific discoveries. But he believes that there is a logic of justification; namely, we establish that the discoveries are genuine by whether or not they survive severe tests aimed at refuting them. In the view of the present authors, the distinction is sometimes useful as a crude tool but in fact oversimplifies matters; discovery and justificatory processes take place together and cannot be meaningfully separated—a researcher is always evaluating data, evaluating his or her procedures, deciding what to keep and what to abandon, and so forth. In short, discovery and justification rarely occur sequentially.

Second, it is not the case that positivists must always advocate the use of the experimental method (as opposed to observational case studies, for example); and conversely, it is not the case that anyone who advocates conducting experiments thereby is a positivist. Experiments are unsurpassed for disentangling factors that might be causally involved in producing some effect and for establishing that some factor is indeed acting as a cause. Any researchers—of whatever philosophical or epistemological conviction, and not just positivists—might find themselves embroiled in a problem that would benefit from their obtaining insight into the causal factors at work in that context; but it is also the case that there are many research situations in which an experiment is not appropriate, for a positivist or anyone else. Thus, an experiment would not be appropriate if you wanted to determine what beliefs a teacher held about a particular classroom incident that you had observed; but an experiment might be relevant if you wanted to determine which factors were causally responsible for a two-minute skit on the television program *Sesame Street* producing the high degree of focused concentration that you had noticed in young viewers. Without an experiment, you could not say definitively what was responsible for their interest—the shortness of the skit, the content, the number and nature of the characters involved (puppets, or a puppet and a person, for instance), the voices, the type of humor involved (slapstick versus verbal), the presence of you as an observer, the characteristics of the particular children who were viewing the skit, or an interaction among several of these factors. But a series of studies in which these factors were systematically altered might settle the matter and yield information that was useful for individuals planning to produce other educational programs for that particular age-group. There is nothing particularly positivistic about the use of the experimental method here. (In fact it is a method we use in a rough-and-ready way in ordinary contexts all the time; for instance, when we pull out and then replace, one by one, the cables at the back of our stereo system to find out which one is causing a buzzing sound.) As Donald Campbell and Julian Stanley put it in their authoritative handbook on experimental designs, they were "committed to the experiment: as the only means for settling disputes regarding educational practice, as the only way of verifying educational improvements, and as the only way of establishing a cumulative tradition in which improvements can be introduced without the danger of a faddish discard of old wisdom in favor of inferior novelties" (Campbell and Stanley 1966, 2). It should be noted that in addition to being a psychologist, Campbell was an able philosopher who strongly opposed positivism.

A third, and somewhat related, misconception is that positivists can be recognized by their adherence to the use of quantitative data and statistical analyses. A positivist believes, as Skinner put it, that researchers must avoid the "inferred" and move instead to the "observed" (or observable) and in general must avoid using terms that in the long run cannot be defined by expressions that refer only to observables or to physical operations or manipulations. *It should be evident that there is nothing here that identifies positivists with the use of quantitative data and statistics.* And, as before, neither is the converse true—nonpositivists are free to use quantitative data and statistical analyses if their research problems call for these methods. In fact, many statistical models rely on probabilistic relations (relations of tendencies and likelihoods) and not on the mechanistic conception of reality that some early positivists held.

There is a fourth charge that at first might seem a little abstract but is nevertheless of some interest given recent debates in the research community. Positivists are often charged with being *realists* (another general term of abuse) in that they are said to believe that there is an "ultimate reality," not only in the physical realm but also in the world of human affairs; it is the aim of science to describe and explain this one "reality" accurately and objectively. Yet a number of people these days believe that what is accepted as real depends on the theoretical or cultural framework in which the investigator is located; there are thus multiple "realities," not one ultimate or absolute reality. We shall have more to say about this matter later; sensible people have different views on this, and indeed the coauthors of this volume have some disagreements over the various issues that arise here. (For an overview of the issues, see Phillips 1992, chap. 5.)

The problem is that this account of positivism is just about the opposite of the truth. If there is an ultimate reality, it is clear that (at least in the view of the positivists) we do not have direct observational contact with it, which is highlighted by the fact that philosophers often call the belief in an ultimate reality *"metaphysical* realism" (see, for example, Searle 1995). And, as should be clear

again from the passages by Skinner that were quoted, positivists (especially those
at the logical positivist end of the spectrum) are far from embracing metaphysical theories such as this. For most positivists, the only thing that matters is what
we *are* in contact with, namely, our sense experience, and they accept that it is
meaningless to make independent claims about the "reality" to which these experiences "refer" or "correspond." (Technically, most positivists are more accurately described as adherents of phenomenalism or sensationalism rather than
realism.)

## PROBLEMS WITH FOUNDATIONALIST EPISTEMOLOGIES

A strong argument can be made that during the second half of the twentieth century the long reign of the foundationalist epistemologies (including positivism)
came to an end (although the surviving adherents of empiricism and rationalism
of course would not agree). It is important to realize, however, that experience
and reason have not been shown to be irrelevant to the production of human
knowledge; rather, the realization has grown that there are severe problems fac-
ing anyone who would still maintain that these are the solid or indubitable *foundations* of our knowledge. Before turning to an exposition of the new
*nonfoundationalist epistemology*, and in particular the form of it that has traditionally been labeled as "postpositivism," we need to give an account of the difficulties (findings and arguments) that led to this dethronement. In so doing we
shall be "debunking" some traditional shibboleths about the nature of science and
laying the foundation for the claim we shall make later that a more open and less
doctrinaire account of the nature of science needs to be given.

There are six main issues that are extremely troublesome for foundationalists:
the relativity of "the light of reason," the theory-laden nature of perception, the
underdetermination of theory by evidence, the "Duhem-Quine" thesis and the role
of auxiliary assumptions in scientific reasoning, the problem of induction, and
the growing recognition of the fact that scientific inquiry is a social activity. These
will be discussed in turn.

### The Relativity of the "Light of Reason"

This issue need not detain us for very long, because it is pretty obvious (!) that
what is obvious to one person may not be obvious to another. What is indubitable and self-evident depends on one's background and intellectual proclivities
and is hardly a solid basis on which to build a whole edifice about knowledge.
In the ancient world, Scipio evidently thought the following argument was self-
evidently true, whereas we think it is obviously deficient: "Animals, which move,
have limbs and muscles. The earth does not have limbs and muscles; therefore it
does not move." The ancient mathematician Euclid formalized geometry by set-

ting it out as a series of deductions (proofs) starting from a few premises (assumptions or postulates) that he took to be self-evident or themselves needing no proof; but the history of the field in the past two centuries has been one in which questions *have* been raised about some of these premises—leading to the development of non-Euclidean geometries and also to new discussions of the nature of mathematical proof itself. Even Descartes's famous premise "I think, therefore I am" has been shown to be more involved than he believed. Where, for example, does the notion of an "I" or self come from? (In fact, the important term "cogito" that he used, in which the verb form implies that there is an actor, is only true of the conjugations in certain languages. In other languages it is not even possible to say "I think." Descartes tried to doubt everything, but he forgot to doubt his own language!) Hans Reichenbach makes a similar point about Descartes and then adds

> It was the search for certainty which made this excellent mathematician drift into such muddled logic. It seems that the search for certainty can make a man blind to the postulates of logic, that the attempt to base knowledge on reason alone can make him abandon the principles of cogent reasoning. (Reichenbach 1953, 36)

None of these examples is meant to suggest that we should not use our rational faculties; rather, they show that caution and modesty are called for. Sometimes our reason is defective or the premises upon which our faculty of reason operates are not so strong and indubitable as we suppose.

## Theory-Laden Perception

It is crucial for the empiricist (including positivist) branch of foundationalism that perception or observation be the solid, indubitable basis on which knowledge claims are erected and that it also serves as the neutral or disinterested court of appeal that adjudicates between rival claims. It has become clear, however, that observation is not "neutral" in the requisite sense.

Earlier this century a number of prominent philosophers, including Ludwig Wittgenstein, Karl Popper, and N. R. Hanson argued that observation is theory-laden: What an observer sees, and also what he or she does not see, and the form that the observation takes, is influenced by the background knowledge of the observer—the theories, hypotheses, assumptions, or conceptual schemes that the observer harbors. A simple example or two should make this clear. One of the coauthors of this book had rarely seen a game of basketball played until after his migration to the United States from Australia in his mid-thirties. When one of his graduate students took him to his first professional game, all that he could see were tall men racing up and down the court bouncing and throwing the ball. Remarks from his companion like "Did you see that terrific move?" were met with a blank stare. To notice a few selected movements on court out of all the movements taking place there and to see them as constituting a "terrific move" requires some prior knowledge of basketball—enough, at least, to be able to know what constitutes a skilled "move" and what doesn't, and enough to be able to disregard the irrelevant actions taking place on the court at that moment. To restore the ego of our coauthor, however, it should be noted that he has been a conjuror since childhood, and at a professional magic performance or when watching magicians on television he can see "moves" that other members of the audience do not notice! Similarly, someone who has had classroom experience can often see things happening that another observer without that background cannot or does not. "There is," as Hanson put it, "more to seeing than meets the eyeball" (Hanson 1958, 7).

It is worth clarifying that the coauthor was not suffering from poor eyesight. His brain was probably registering (if only briefly) the complex plays happening on the basketball court (although we must be careful here, for human perception is not quite like a mental video recording). But he did not *notice* certain things, and so he described what was happening differently from his student, who knew the significance of certain things and so saw and described the events differently (a description that also drew heavily on basketball "jargon," or terminology). But our hero knows, from long experience, that anyone watching a magic show has to be alert to the magician's stratagem of "misdirection"—a technique whereby the magician, either through words or actions or the use of interesting props such as bright silk scarves or attractive assistants, leads members of the audience to expect a certain thing to happen; they focus their attention on what they expect, and they don't notice where the really significant action is taking place (the magician's left hand retrieving a pigeon from a holder under the bottom of his jacket, for example).

Another case might be helpful. One of us was conducting a class in which the teaching assistant was a dedicated Freudian who had worked in a school for schizophrenic children; a student taking the class was an advanced doctoral student with a strong background in behaviorist psychology. The topic of autism came up, and the instructor decided to show a short film that featured a young autistic woman who had been treated and apparently "cured." The behaviorist and the Freudian had held opposing theories about the nature of autism, and hence they also strongly disagreed about the efficacy of the treatment described in the film. The class viewed the film with the sound track turned down as the two of them stood on either side of the screen and gave rival commentaries. There was an amazing disparity—they noticed quite different things (often ignoring events and features that the other pointed to as being significant), and of course they used quite different terminology to speak about what they were seeing. What they were seeing, how they described it, and also what they didn't see or pay attention to, all seemed to be directly influenced by the different theories and assumptions they were bringing with them. There was *no* "theory neutral" observational "court of appeal" that could be appealed to in order to settle beyond all possibility of argument the differences between them.

## The Underdetermination of Theory by Evidence

This difficulty to some extent overlaps the one described above; it is another "nail in the coffin" of all forms of empiricist foundationalism. Put starkly, we cannot claim that observational or other evidence unequivocally supports a particular theory or fully warrants the claim that it is true because there are many other (indeed, a potentially infinite number of other) theories that also are compatible with this same body of evidence (and can thereby claim to be warranted by it). More pithily, theory is *underdetermined* by evidence—which is a severe blow to the view that our knowledge is "founded" on sense experience.

This can be demonstrated most simply by means of a couple of diagrams. Suppose that we have performed a study and have collected some data points that can be graphed as follows (let us use X and Y as the axes representing the two factors in which we are interested) (See Figure 1.2.)

It might be supposed that these points support the "theory" that the relationship between X and Y is a linear one that can be depicted by a straight line. (See Figure 1.3.)

But, in fact, there are infinitely many curves that can be drawn to fit these three data points, just two of which are depicted in Figure 1.4.

The fact of the matter is that the three points *underdetermine* the shape of the curve/line (i.e., in effect the nature of the theory) that we can hypothesize "fits" them. Nor is the situation helped if a fourth or even a fifth point (or more) is added. Even if these new points happen to fit the straight line, the matter is not settled, for although one or maybe both the curves depicted above will be shown

**Figure 1.2. Data about X and Y**

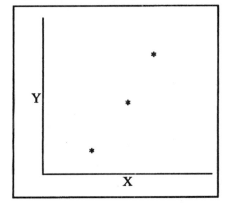

**Figure 1.3.   One Possible Relationship**

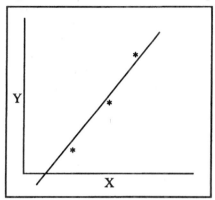

to be incorrect, an infinite group of other more intricate curves will remain compatible with the newly extended set of data points. We might hold beliefs or accept criteria that persuade us that the line is the correct hypothesis, for example;
we might have the assumption that nature is simple (although we would also need
to make the assumption that lines are geometrically simpler than curves). But then,
obviously, it is not the observational data *alone* that are determining what hypothesis we will accept. (It is worth noting that an issue touched upon earlier is
relevant to this example: All the points that are being graphed have to be accepted
by the researchers concerned as being genuine data; of course, the new data points
might be rejected as "outliers" or simply as erroneous or "artifacts." When new
information does not fit your theory, which do you doubt first: the long-standing
theory or the new information?)

The point that there is a gap separating the observation of a phenomenon from
the forming of an explanation or theory or hypothesis about it can be made in
another way—the gap cannot be bridged without help *from outside the observed*

**Figure 1.4.   Other Possible Relationships**

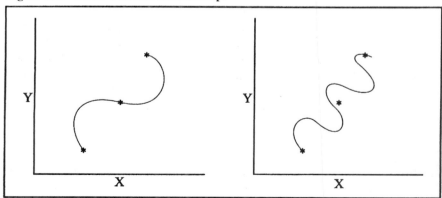

*phenomenon itself*! A phenomenon does not have associated with it anything that determines that we must conceptualize or describe it in a particular way—many possible alternative descriptions always exist. In the phraseology favored by philosophers of social science, a phenomenon exists under different descriptions, and it might be easier to explain when placed under one description rather than another. Consider an example that could easily arise during a classroom observation session: A teacher is confronting a student in the class and is pushing her with a relentless series of rather curt questions about the subject matter of last night's homework. The first thing to note is that even this description of the phenomenon is not theory neutral—why did we describe it in terms of "confronting" and "pushing," or "curt" and "relentless"? We could also describe what happened in terms of the language of "interaction" or "dialogue"—there was an extended interaction or dialogue in which the teacher asked a series of difficult questions and so on. Perhaps we could describe what happened in terms of the teacher venting her anger or hostility on the student, or we could describe it as the teacher acting out an oppressive power relation, or we could describe it in terms of the teacher trying to motivate the unwilling student by asking her a series of challenging questions about the homework. One of the problems here is that we, the classroom observers, are probably approaching the situation with hypotheses or background theories already in mind that color our observations (for, as we have seen, all observation is theory-laden); perhaps we were told by the principal of the school that the teacher is an unpleasant and unsympathetic person, and the description given above was written from that perspective. The point is that whatever occurred in the classroom took place without labels attached. We, the observers, provide the labels, and we have a wide range from which to choose. And the way we describe the phenomenon is related to the way we will explain it—a teacher being curt and even victimizing a student is explained differently from a teacher challenging a student to "be all that she can be"! (Philosopher Bertrand Russell somewhere used this example, which makes the same general point: "I am firm, you are stubborn, and he is a pig-headed fool." These are three labels that describe the identical character trait of "sticking to your opinions," but they are labels that embody quite different theories and evaluations of the trait. The phenomenon itself is "neutral" with respect to these evaluative descriptions. Another example widely used by philosophers is the observation that a person's arm rises; is this to be described as a twitch, as a salute, or as the asking of a question? The choice of the description will be made by considering more than just the sight of the arm moving; it will involve many other assumptions or judgments about context, intent, and cultural conventions—just the sorts of things Skinner would advise us to ignore!)

## The Duhem-Quine Thesis and Auxiliary Assumptions

The so-called Duhem-Quine thesis, named in honor of the two philosophers who formulated it, also presents a problem for empiricists who believe that evidence (observational data or measurements) serves unproblematically as a solid and indubitable basis for our knowledge. The thesis can best be explained in terms of an analogy. Think of all your knowledge, of all the theories you accept, as being interrelated and as forming one large network; this whole network is present whenever you make observations or collect data. Now suppose that you are carrying out a test of some hypothesis and you find a recalcitrant piece of data that apparently refutes this. Do you have to abandon or at least change the now challenged hypothesis? Not at all; certainly you have to make some accommodating change somewhere, but perhaps the problem is not with your hypothesis but with some other part of your network of beliefs. To test your hypothesis you may have accepted some other data, then made calculations on this, then used instrumentation of some sort to set up the test of the prediction you have made. The error could well have entered somewhere during this complex process. (There is a danger here—an unscrupulous researcher could use this line of argument to protect his or her favorite hypotheses or theories from refutation during tests by always laying the blame on something else.) The point of the Duhem-Quine thesis is that evidence relates to all of the network of beliefs, not just to one isolated part; all of our beliefs are "up for grabs" during the test of any one of them—we can save one assumption or belief if we are willing to jettison another one.

Whenever we carry out a study, test some hypothesis, or explore an issue, we make use of various parts of our background knowledge (the extended network) that we are taking to be unproblematic at least for the purposes of the particular inquiry that we are engaged upon at present. Thus we may make use of measuring devices or tests or interview questions, on the assumption that they are sound; we might use various types of statistical analyses, making the same assumption about these techniques. These (temporarily unproblematic) items of background knowledge or of established techniques have been called "auxiliaries" or "auxiliary assumptions." Thus, when we test hypotheses and try to extend the domain of our present knowledge, the phenomena do not "speak for themselves"; in fact we are trying to determine what to make of them, using these auxiliaries as tools in the process. So much for the key "foundational" thesis of empiricism!

The use of auxiliaries is particularly relevant for understanding the logic of testing our hypotheses, which is an important way in which we provide warrants for them. Hypotheses that survive strong tests might not be true, but certainly surviving a series of tests is much more to their credit than failing. The traditional account of testing (sometimes called "the hypothetico-deductive method") is as follows: Suppose that "H" is the hypothesis that we are testing and "P" is the prediction we deduce from this hypothesis. If H is true, we predict P will be found to be true, and we collect data to test this prediction. If P is not found to be borne out, then H must be false. (Extra credit: Logicians call this form of argument "modus tollens"!) We can represent the logical syllogism in this way:

IF H, THEN P
<u>                        NOT P</u>
THEREFORE NOT H

Or in terms of an example:

> If this student is at Kohlberg's stage 5, then she will answer X when
> interviewed.
> <u>She did not answer X.</u>
> Therefore she is not at Kohlberg's stage 5.

However, this account omits the presence of the auxiliaries that were used in
carrying out the test; a more accurate description of the situation is the following (using "A" to represent the auxiliary premises or assumptions):

IF H *AND* A, THEN P
<u>                        NOT P</u>
THEREFORE NOT (H *OR* A)

This is a valid piece of reasoning, but unfortunately it is not as helpful as we might
have wished. If a test is negative, we cannot conclude that the hypothesis is incorrect, for the error might lie somewhere in the auxiliaries; we can only conclude that there is an error somewhere in the conjunction "H and A." In terms of
the example,

> If this student is at Kohlberg's stage 5, and if the interview questions are an
> accurate way to measure Kohlberg's stages, and if the student is answering
> honestly, and so forth, then she will answer X when interviewed.
> <u>She did not answer X.</u>
> Therefore, either she is not at Kohlberg's stage 5, or the interview questions
> were not an accurate way to determine what stage she was at, or she was
> not answering honestly, etc.

For the record, it should be noted that positive tests never establish that H is
true, for the form of argument involved is a fallacy. (More extra credit: Logicians
call this "affirming the consequent"!):

IF H, THEN P
<u>                        P</u>
THEREFORE H

Or in terms of the example:

> If this student is at Kohlberg's stage 5, and if (the auxiliaries), then she will
> answer X when she is interviewed.
> <u>She answered X.</u>
> Therefore she is at Kohlberg's stage 5.

It is easy to see that this is invalid; she might have gotten the answer by guessing or by accident, or perhaps people other than those at stage 5 also can give this answer.

Thus no number of positive instances necessarily *proves* a particular theory or hypothesis because any finite set of data can be accounted for in more than one way; conversely, no number of disconfirming instances necessarily *disproves* a particular theory or hypothesis because we can modify or reject some other part of our belief system to explain away the apparently disconfirming instances. These points seem to support the relativistic view that there is no way a theory or hypothesis can be either proven or disproven and thus one theory is as good as another! We will argue later that the failure of the hard positivistic account of what constitutes proof does not, however, need to lead us to completely denigrate hypothesis formation and testing; postpositivism simply approaches such matters with a more modest and less foundationalist set of aspirations.

## The Problem of Induction

This is the longest-standing issue for empiricists, with a lively history of discussion going back about two and a half centuries to the work of the Scottish philosopher David Hume. Put simply, the problem is this: How do we know that phenomena that we have not experienced will resemble those that we have experienced in the past? Our knowledge would be limited in usefulness if it only applied to cases in which we already have evidence that our claims are true. All of us, empiricists or not, often wish to apply our knowledge to new or prospective cases; we wish to make plans, to order our lives, to make rational predictions, to intervene in social or educational affairs to effect improvements. We wish to use our understanding of gravity, for instance, which is based on our experience observing phenomena on the earth and in the solar system and nearby universe, to understand events that took place in the early life of the universe or are happening at present inside black holes (both these classes of phenomena, of course, being unobservable to us). We expect that airplanes, which have flown in the past, will continue to fly in virtue of the fact that the forces of nature that enabled flight to take place up until now will continue to operate in the same ways. We wish to take treatments of learning disorders that were proven to be efficacious in past studies and use them in cases tomorrow. Or, to use Hume's more homely example, "The bread which I formerly ate nourished me. . . . But does it follow that other bread must also nourish me at another time . . . ?" (Hume 1955, 48).

What entitles us to be sanguine about our prospects of applying our understandings (our currently *warranted* understandings) to new cases? What observations have we made that enable us to be certain about as yet unobserved cases? Hume's skeptical conclusion about these matters has rung out through the years; referring to the question of whether it follows that in future bread will continue to be nourishing to humans, he said tersely, "The consequence seems nowise necessary" (p. 48). And, of course, as an empiricist Hume seems to have been justified in holding this opinion for, if our knowledge is based *solely* on experience, we cannot have knowledge about things that we have *not* experienced! Hume concluded that (to use modern terminology) we are more or less conditioned; we get into the habit of expecting that a past regularity or uniformity will hold in the future, simply because it held true in all relevant cases in the past. We have eaten bread so often that we simply expect (as a matter of *psychological* accustomization) that it will be edible and nutritious in the future. But this expectation is not *logically* justified.

The logical issue is as follows: Apparently we make inductions in which we extend our knowledge beyond the evidence available, but induction is not a logically compelling form of reasoning, as the following makes clear:

A (1) HAS CHARACTERISTIC X
A (2) HAS CHARACTERISTIC X
A (3) HAS CHARACTERISTIC X

. . .

A (N) HAS CHARACTERISTIC X
THEREFORE ALL A's HAVE CHARACTERISTIC X

No matter how many cases of "A" we observe to have characteristic X, no matter how large the "N" happens to be, it does not follow logically that *all* cases of A will have this characteristic; we are making an inductive leap beyond the evidence we have available, and there is no certainty about our conclusion. This is illustrated in logic texts by the classic example that warms the heart of our coauthor from Australia: All the very many swans observed in Europe up until the settlement of Australia were found to be white, so the inductive conclusion had been drawn that all swans were white, and this "obviously true" inductive generalization was often used in textbooks; unfortunately for this induction, when Europeans arrived in western Australia, they discovered black swans on what they came to call, appropriately enough, the Swan River! (We should note here, echoing a previous discussion, that one possible response could have been—and indeed was—that these creatures were not swans; in other words, the previous generalization could have been protected!)

Insofar as inductive reasoning has been regarded as fairly central in science, the "problem of induction" has seemed something of a disgrace. Science is a prime example of human knowledge, yet it centrally involves a form of reasoning that is not logically compelling! So philosophers of science and logicians have been much exercised to find a solution. Some, like Karl Popper, have denied that inductive reasoning is important in science; indeed, Popper denied that it exists at all. (He believed that we misdescribe the pattern of reasoning we use and mistakenly suppose it to be inductive, when really we should regard our collecting evidence about A1, A2, and so on as a series of independent tests of the hypothesis that "all A have X"; he rejected the view that our observations concerning A1, A2, and so on were the foundational observations from which we induced the conclusion that "all A have X.") Others accept the fact that induction is not deductively valid, and so its conclusions are not certain, but argue that inductive reasoning at least makes the conclusions we reach *probable.* The fact that N cases have been found in which an A has characteristic X (and that no cases observed so far lack X) does not establish that all cases of A have X; but this fact makes the conclusion that "all A have X" to some degree probable. However, there are two problems here: How can this probability be calculated? And does probability provide a strong enough foundation on which empiricists can erect the whole edifice of our scientific knowledge?

Some philosophers and scientists favor a slightly different "Bayesian" approach, in which new evidence that an A has characteristic X reduces the prior uncertainty that we had about all cases of A having X (an approach that uses a theorem of probability theory derived in the eighteenth century by Thomas Bayes). This was the path favored by Hans Reichenbach, who clearly recognized that "Hume's problem" required a recasting of empiricism, for he wrote that the "classical period of empiricism . . . ends with the breakdown of empiricism; for that is what Hume's analysis of induction amounts to" (Reichenbach 1953, 89). His Bayesian probabilistic approach becomes clear a little later:

> A set of observational facts will always fit more than one theory; in other words, there are several theories from which these facts can be derived. The inductive inference is used to confer upon each of these theories a degree of probability, and the most probable theory is then accepted. . . . The detective tries to determine the most probable explanation. His considerations follow established rules of probability; using all factual clues and all his knowledge of human psychology, he attempts to arrive at conclusions, which in turn are tested by new observations specifically planned for this purpose. Each test, based on new material, increases or decreases the probability of the explanation; but never can the explanation constructed be regarded as absolutely certain. (Reichenbach 1953, 232)

Here Reichenbach is moving from logical positivism to present-day nonfoundationalist postpositivism!

Despite the attractiveness of the position of Reichenbach and others on this matter, it is safe to say that there is no unanimity about how to resolve "Hume's problem"—even postpositivists disagree amongst themselves over this issue.

## The Social Nature of Scientific Research

The classic empiricists (and for that matter rationalists as well) did not make much of the obvious fact that researchers belong to a community; Locke's account, for example, was phrased in very individualistic terms—the inquirer individually constructs complex ideas from his or her stock of simple ideas, which have their origin and justification in that particular individual's experience. The empiricist can, of course, acknowledge that an individual scientist interacts with colleagues while on the path to formulating a new item of knowledge, but the decision about the content of the knowledge claim is always, for the empiricist, driven solely by the sense experiences that serve as the foundation for that claim. Since the publication of Thomas S. Kuhn's important book *The Structure of Scientific Revolutions* (Kuhn 1962), however, there has been a growing acknowledgment of the fact that the community to which the scientist belongs (a community that is united around a framework, or *paradigm*) plays a more central role in determining what evidence is acceptable, what criteria and methods are to be used, what form a theory should take, and so forth. These things are not simply determined by "neutral" sense experience. Kuhn wrote:

> The very existence of science depends upon vesting the power to choose between paradigms in the members of a special kind of community. . . . [The members of this group] may not, however, be drawn at random from society as a whole, but is rather the well-defined community of the scientist's professional compeers. . . . What better criterion than the decision of the scientific group could there be? (Kuhn 1962, 166–169)

And it is not only choice between paradigms; choices made within paradigms also are a matter for communal decision. Kuhn states that the solutions to problems within the framework that are put forward by the individual scientist cannot "be merely personal but must instead be accepted as solutions by many" (Kuhn 1962, 167).

The point that subsequent scholars have developed is that decisions made within groups—even professional groups of scientists—are influenced by much more than the "objective facts." In a broad sense, "political" factors can be seen to play a role, for in a group some people will of necessity have more power or influence than others, some will have their voices repressed, some individuals will have much more at stake than others (their reputations or economic gains, for instance), and some will be powerfully motivated by ideologies or religious convictions. As the editors of the volume *Feminist Epistemologies* put it, "The work presented here supports the hypothesis that politics intersect traditional epistemology. . . . [These essays] raise a question about the adequacy of any account of knowledge that ignores the politics involved in knowledge" (Alcoff and Potter 1993, 13). This is a long way from the vision of how scientific knowledge is built up that was held by Locke, Comte, and Bridgman. It remains to be seen to what degree postpositivists can accommodate this social perspective.

## CONCLUSION

The new approach of postpositivism was born in an intellectual climate in which these six problems confronting foundational epistemologies had become widely recognized. This new position is an "orientation," not a unified "school of thought," for there are many issues on which postpositivists disagree. But they are united in believing that human knowledge is not based on unchallengeable, rock-solid foundations—it is *conjectural*. We have grounds, or warrants, for asserting the beliefs, or conjectures, that we hold as scientists, often very good grounds, but these grounds are not indubitable. Our warrants for accepting these things can be withdrawn in the light of further investigation. Philosopher of science Karl Popper, a key figure in the development of nonfoundationalist postpositivism, put it well when he wrote, "But what, then, are the sources of our knowledge? The answer, I think, is this: there are all kinds of sources of our knowledge, but *none has authority*." Thus the empiricist's questions, 'How do you know? What is the source of your assertion?', are wrongly put. They are not formulated in an inexact or slovenly manner, but *they are entirely misconceived*: they are questions that beg for an authoritarian answer" (Popper 1965, 24–25; emphasis in original).

## REFERENCES

Alcoff, L., and E. Potter. 1993. *Feminist Epistemologies*. New York: Routledge.

Ashby, R. W. 1964. "Logical Positivism." In *A Critical History of Western Philosophy*. Edited by D. J. O'Connor. New York: Free Press.

Campbell, D., and J. Stanley. 1966. *Experimental and Quasi-Experimental Designs for Research*. Chicago: Rand McNally.

Comte, A. [1830] 1970. *Introduction to Positive Philosophy*. Translated by Frederick Ferre. Indianapolis: Bobbs-Merrill.

Curtis, C., and F. Greenslet, eds. 1962. *The Practical Cogitator*. Boston: Houghton Mifflin.

Descartes, R. [1641] 1953. *Meditations on the First Philosophy*. In *A Discourse on Method*. Edited and translated by Joh Veitch. London: Dent/Everyman Library.

Dewey, J. [1938] 1966. *Logic: The Theory of Inquiry*. New York: Holt, Rinehart & Winston.

Hanson, N. R. 1958. *Patterns of Discovery*. Cambridge: Cambridge University Press.

Hume, D. [1748] 1955. *An Inquiry concerning Human Understanding*. New York: Macmillan.

Kuhn, T. S. 1962. *The Structure of Scientific Revolutions*. Chicago: University of Chicago Press.

Locke, J. [1690] 1959. *An Essay concerning Human Understanding*. London: Dent/Everyman Library.

Phillips, D. C. 1992. *The Social Scientist's Bestiary*. Oxford: Pergamon.

Phillips, D. C. 1994. "Positivism, Antipositivism, and Empiricism." In *International Encyclopedia of Education*. Edited by T. Husen and N. Postlethwaite. 2d. ed. Oxford: Pergamon.

Phillips, D. C. 1998. "How, Why, What, When, and Where: Perspectives on Constructivism in Psychology and Education." *Issues in Education* 3, no. 2: 151–194.

Popper, K. 1965. *Conjectures and Refutations*. 2d ed. New York: Basic.

Reichenbach, H. 1953. *The Rise of Scientific Philosophy*. Berkeley: University of California Press.

Searle, J. 1995. *The Construction of Social Reality*. New York: Free Press.

Skinner, B. F. 1953. *Science and Human Behavior*. New York: Free Press.

Skinner, B. F. 1972. *Beyond Freedom and Dignity*. London: Jonathan Cape.

Winokur, J. 1987. *The Portable Curmudgeon*. New York: New American Library.

# 2

## Philosophical Commitments of Postpositivist Researchers

> There are no ultimate sources of knowledge. Every source, every suggestion, is welcome; and every source, every suggestion, is open to critical examination. . . . The proper epistemological question is not one about sources; rather, we ask whether the assertion made is true—that is to say, whether it agrees with the facts. . . . And we try to find this out, as well as we can, by examining or testing the assertion itself; either in a direct way, or by examining or testing its consequences.
>
> Karl Popper

In chapter 1 we attempted to clarify what postpositivism *is not*: it is not a form of foundationalism, and so it is not a form of rationalism or of empiricism (and thus is not a form of positivism). Postpositivism is a *nonfoundationalist* approach to human knowledge that rejects the view that knowledge is erected on absolutely secure foundations—for there are no such things; postpositivists accept *fallibilism* as an unavoidable fact of life. As Catherine Elgin has put it,

> If the fallibility of induction is a manifestation of our general epistemological predicament, our best methods for securing knowledge are apt occasionally to fail. They may, like a hung jury, yield no verdict, leaving us in ignorance about the matter at hand. But sometimes they do worse. In counting undetected errors as knowledge, they yield false positives. Although there remains a presumption in favor of their products, these procedures, being fallible, are not intrinsically reliable. Still, the procedures we employ are the best ones available. (Elgin 1996, 11)

In short, the postpositivist sees knowledge as *conjectural*. These conjectures are supported by the strongest (if possibly imperfect) warrants we can muster at the time and are always subject to reconsideration. In the course of our discussion in chapter 1 we started to clarify the contemporary philosophical view of the nature of science by showing how, as this understanding emerged, it presented serious problems for positivism and other foundationalist positions. The epigraph at the beginning of this chapter is taken from Karl Popper's *Conjectures and Refutations* (1965, 27)—a book whose title brilliantly captures the essence of his nonfoundationalism and summarizes, more or less, our exposition in chapter 1.

No doubt the discussion thus far has raised more issues than it has settled about the commitments of postpositivists. It would be sensible for us to tackle these questions, doubts, and uncertainties head-on: if postpositivists are not positivists, then what do they believe? In the following pages we draw upon our experience dealing with skeptical colleagues and graduate students (many of whom have been educational researchers of various kinds rather than philosophers), and so we will formulate—and address as forthrightly as possible—the most common issues that have been raised, questions that cluster around a couple of vital and controversial topics. A point made earlier needs to be reemphasized at the outset, however: postpositivism is not a unitary school of thought. It is not like a political party or a narrow sect whose members all think alike. Thus the way we deal with these issues will not necessarily reflect how all postpositivists would reply.


## HOW CAN KNOWLEDGE NOT HAVE A FOUNDATION?

*Question:* It still is not fully clear how, on the postpositivist account, knowledge can be built up when there are no authoritative sources—when, as Popper said, "every source" is welcome but none is authoritative. Can this be discussed in more detail, with an example?

*Response:* Popper made the point that when we are faced with a "knowledge claim" that we are asked to accept, generally we ask ourselves if it is likely to be true, given what we know about the evidence, the "facts" of the case; often we test the assertion for ourselves or examine with a critical eye the tests that have already been carried out. In short, we look at the warrants that are adduced to support both the knowledge claim and the purported facts that support it. Thus we look at the evidence that was offered, the arguments that were made, and the calculations, controlled experiments, interviews, and so forth that were carried out and can be marshaled in favor of the claim. We also look at criticisms and counterarguments and negative analyses. If necessary, we plan a crucial experiment or study of our own, or we do a literature review and read about other studies that might be relevant. Then we make up our minds and develop a case—but with the realization that at some later date we might come across pertinent evidence or criticism that forces us to change our mind.

Popper's words suggest that the nonfoundationalist, in judging whether a claim is warranted or not, is not concerned about where the claim *came from*—about who formulated the claim or conjecture or when or what their psychological or political or other motivations were for putting it forward (we might, of course, be interested in these things on other grounds) If the conjecture or claim is interesting and captures our attention, we examine first not the history of its origin but the case for it. In Dewey's terms, we examine the warrant for the claim, and if it is strong we accept the claim, with the awareness that the warrant might later be withdrawn. (Of course, if the source of a claim is a person we suspect of bias or of having a hidden agenda, this might tip us off as to the possible failings of the evidentiary support for the claim; but we must examine this evidence. It is important to remember that a researcher may have a bias or a hidden agenda while making an assertion that is nonetheless well warranted.)

The analogy of the detective in the quotation from Reichenbach that we mentioned toward the end of the previous chapter is helpful here (Elgin also used a similar analogy). The case we build up for a knowledge claim is always *circumstantial*; in police work circumstantial evidence is often the only evidence available, and it frequently happens that it is substantial enough to warrant action (an arrest, a trial, and a conviction). But there are cases in which the decision reached on such a basis eventually turned out to be faulty (a new set of DNA tests might be carried out or the real criminal might make a deathbed confession that is backed up with evidence). The original (and now rejected) claim was, at the time, the best that could be made, and it was warranted then—but not *absolutely* warranted. This acceptance of the possible imperfection and fallibility of evidence is one of the central tenets of postpositivism, but it does not entail that we have to give up the idea that evidence is pertinent to our judgments about the truth or warrantability of our conjectures.

Surely there can be little doubt that this process has been illustrated time and again throughout the course of human intellectual history. Astronomers at one time were warranted in believing that there were only seven planets orbiting the sun, and biologists for several decades up until the late 1950s were warranted in believing that there were forty-eight chromosomes in the nucleus of each human cell (excepting the germ cells). In each case new work undercut the old warrants—two new planets were discovered, and careful lab work showed that there were only forty-six human chromosomes. It seems that this process of making knowledge claims and then refining or abandoning some of them for claims that are more strongly warranted is a pattern that is better described within a nonfoundationalist framework than in a foundationalist one (since the latter frame has to explain why claims made on supposedly indubitable foundations so often have turned out to be false). As one of the present authors often notes in class, if the history of science proves anything, it is that all theories turn out eventually to be wrong (even if "wrong" only means incomplete or standing in need of elaboration).

*Question:* Before you go on to discuss an example drawn from educational research, your remarks raise two interrelated concerns: (1) If knowledge claims can
always be overthrown, if as you put it our warrants for asserting our beliefs can
be withdrawn, why should we believe or accept *anything*? (2) Doesn't your
nonfoundationalism play into the hands of the postmodernists and social
constructivists who see knowledge construction not as a rational human activity
based on evidence and the use of the "scientific method" but as a social activity
based on the exercise of power, politics, and ideology?

*Response:* These are very pertinent concerns. Probably they are part at least of
what postmodernist Jean-François Lyotard had in mind when he wrote about "in-
credulity towards metanarratives" and "the obsolescence of the metanarrative
apparatus of legitimation" (Lyotard 1984, xxiv). He was making the point that
the overarching story (metanarrative) that has been told to justify or legitimate
belief in science as an epistemological activity is "obsolete." He was certainly
right if what he had in mind was the foundationalist story. The point we are making in our book is that the standard arguments against foundationalism do not
apply to the nonfoundationalist account, but inevitably we must grapple with the
skeptical lines of thought embodied in your two questions. Let us take them in
turn.

   First, part of the answer to the concern that question 1 raises is that we *must*
have some beliefs upon which we are prepared to act, for, while we are alive,
act we must! We need to obtain food and shelter, protect ourselves from disease
and natural disasters, and educate the members of the next generation. We can
act on whim or fancy (not a particularly secure way to ensure our survival in a
rather unforgiving natural environment) or on mere custom or tradition or on the
basis of the best (most tested and otherwise warranted) understandings that our
species has developed, even though they might not be perfect. It can be argued
that it is irrational not to be guided by the best knowledge that is available at the
time, *for currently this knowledge is warranted.* Would it be rational to eat food
contaminated with lead on the grounds that the claim "lead is a deadly poison"
is a fallible one that might at some future time be overthrown? Or to revert to
Hume's example, would it be rational to avoid eating bread on the grounds that
in future it might be found to be unhealthy? (Woody Allen parodied the change-
able nature of human knowledge in his movie *Sleeper*; he played the owner of a
health food store who was revived after being frozen for several hundred years,
only to find that chocolate fudge sundaes were regarded as about the healthiest
food available—people in the twentieth century were terribly wrong, he was told,
to believe these were bad for you! This possibility exists, of course, but nevertheless Woody and the rest of us currently are well advised, on the basis of our
best-warranted knowledge, not to eat too many of them.)

   Since both authors have lived in California for many years, earthquake precautions can serve as an analogy. If we were completely skeptical, we might ar-

gue that it is silly to take precautions, to upgrade building codes and the like as new knowledge becomes available, for further knowledge will always eventually be forthcoming. A nonfoundationalist, however, would be likely to argue that the current codes are based on our best understanding of how to produce homes that will suffer less damage than otherwise in an earthquake; new research might or might not turn up other, better understandings, but at present there is evidence that homes constructed to these codes will be more secure than homes that are not. Why, then, is it not rational to build to these current codes?

Your second question essentially asks for our evaluation of the program accepted by sociologists of knowledge (sometimes called "social constructivists"; see Phillips 1997, 1998), that is, the program of explaining the form that our knowledge takes using the explanatory apparatus of sociology and political science. These scholars divide into several different schools. On one hand are moderates who believe that, in addition to the internal considerations that sway knowledge-building communities (the evidence available, the theories that are currently favored, the canons that are accepted concerning the scientific method, and so forth), we also must take into account such things as the relationships of power and influence that occur in all human groups. What emerges as knowledge claims from a community of inquirers bears the stamp of all of these factors. (Who would doubt, for example, that in a laboratory run by a Nobel Prize winner, what is produced by way of "knowledge" has been influenced by the beliefs and desires and so on of the head of the lab, as well as by the evidence or data that are available?) Neither author of this book doubts the validity and usefulness of this moderate kind of sociopolitical study of knowledge production (and we will have a little more to say about knowledge-producing, or epistemic, communities in the following chapter).

On the other hand, however, there is a more radical school, sometimes known as "the strong program in sociology of knowledge" or the "Edinburgh school" (the key early members of the group worked in that city). Their work takes skepticism about the role of evidence to a new level, and they offer a strong or radical attack on the rationality of the scientific enterprise. They seem to deny that what we take to be knowledge is shaped at all by data or evidence or rational considerations of the sort discussed in scientific papers and texts. Instead, the knowledge claims that are made can be accounted for *solely and fully* in sociological terms! As Harry Collins—a member of this school of thought—once put it, "The natural world has a small or nonexistent role in the construction of scientific knowledge" (Collins, quoted in Phillips 1997, 91). Knowledge has the form it does because it is in some people's interests that this be the case; power, influence, economic considerations, and so forth, almost entirely (if not fully) determine what is advanced as knowledge. The present authors reject this "strong" position. We agree that such sociopolitical factors play a role in knowledge production but maintain that "external nature"—the forces and entities and causal mechanisms at work in nature (including in humans and in society)—exerts some

constraint on what we can believe or claim about nature! To foreshadow an example we will make more use of shortly, the real shape of the earth exerts a constraint upon what we can claim about it, and even those who believed the earth
to be flat eventually had to deal with so much counterevidence that no matter
what their personal motivations were, if they were rational they had to come to
terms with its spherical shape. (Nowadays, "flat-earthers" are regarded as cranks.)
For us, all the interesting and important questions arise in the realm between
accepting (1) that evidence underdetermines theory (while it certainly serves as
a constraint against our believing just anything, it still allows room for alternative accounts or interpretations) and (2) that human investigators are always imperfect and situated in social and historical contexts in which multiple motivations operate, and not just a disinterested pursuit of "truth." The practical problem
of formulating reasonable, warranted beliefs or conjectures must be worked out
by balancing these two (for us undeniable) facts.

It is high time for us to return to the request made earlier, to provide a more
in-depth illustration of the nonfoundationalist approach from education-related
research. So consider the example of Lawrence Kohlberg's theory of moral development in children. Kohlberg, working within the broad Piagetian tradition
of invariant stages of intellectual development, claimed that the development of
moral cognition (i.e., the ability to reason about moral problems) also occurs
through a number of stages that form an invariant sequence. He first expounded
this theory, and the evidence for it, in his doctoral dissertation, and the work sur-
vived the examination of his faculty dissertation committee. Soon his ideas were
published, passing the scrutiny of the referees. At that time, then, his theory had
a respectable warrant. Later, however, criticisms were forthcoming (some based
on experimental studies that critics had performed, others based on theoretical
or philosophical grounds), and in response Kohlberg eventually refined the number of stages (from six to seven; he also introduced a transition stage), and he
revised (a number of times) the ways in which he analyzed his interview data—
all these changes being designed to improve his case/warrant, which he also
strengthened with philosophical and other arguments. By this time, Kohlberg had
attracted students and other coworkers; he became the leader of a school of
thought, the full history of which would have to take account of the personality
factors at work, the distribution of power, and so forth. (The developmental
changes in Kohlberg's work are traced in detail, and assessed, in Phillips 1987,
chap. 14.) It is doubtful whether anyone in the educational and psychological
research communities (except perhaps Kohlberg himself, and a handful of his
students and coworkers) regarded his theory as undoubtedly or certainly true, but
many regarded it as probably true. Some, including the present authors, regarded
the counterevidence as indicating that the theory was likely (but not certainly)
false. Eventually one of Kohlberg's colleagues, Carol Gilligan, challenged the
theory on the grounds that he had only studied boys and had excluded girls from
his sample (his assumption evidently had been that the relevant developmental

processes were the same across genders—it is hard to believe today that it took so long for this aspect of Kohlberg's methodology to be challenged). Gilligan offered some data in support of her view that in important ways girls reasoned differently about moral issues (in other words, she challenged this key assumption about gender uniformity). In essence, this wave of criticism undermined, in the judgment of many but not all researchers, the by now complex warrant that Kohlberg and his coworkers had produced for the theory. (Gilligan has written interestingly of her complex relationship with Kohlberg; see Gilligan 1998.)

It should be apparent that this example illustrates the points made in the epigraph by Popper. No one type of data or source was regarded as completely authoritative in this long controversy over Kohlberg's work. Different experimental studies, analytical tools and coding schemes, philosophical arguments, assumptions about normal development and developmental processes, and differences of opinion about what constituted a fair sample of individuals to study all played a role in attempts to produce a convincing warrant and to criticize the ones that were put forward. Some of the "tests" of Kohlberg's work were direct empirical studies, whereas others were more indirect. And no test or argument has been absolutely conclusive; rather, there have been slowly building judgments that his research program either was strong or rather weak. As in a court of law, evidence, counterevidence, arguments, counterarguments, differing assumptions and emotions, legal precedents, and so forth, all play a role. As was seen during the 1994 O. J. Simpson trial, however, these considerations can lead different groups to drastically different—even conflicting—conclusions. And so it is in educational research.

## MULTIPLE BELIEFS, MULTIPLE TRUTHS, MULTIPLE REALITIES

*Question:* It is noteworthy that in your previous answer (and in the earlier discussions) you made use of the notion of "truth." Is this a useful concept these days? Is there such a thing as *truth*? Isn't it rather the case that some people will believe one thing, others will believe something else? You seem to be saying this yourselves. There are multiple truths and hence multiple *realities* as well. In other words, relativism—a term of abuse that, this time, postpositivists often use against their opponents—seems to be the only defensible position.

*Response:* This is a vitally important sequence of questions. But note that it is a sequence—the statement runs together a number of issues that, at least in the first instance, need to be separated out. The issues raised are ones that exercise many people these days, for we live in postmodern times when there is skepticism about general notions like "truth" and "reality," and various types of relativism (e.g., in the epistemological and moral realms) abound. We hope that it is evident from our earlier discussion that *postmodernism* should not be confused with *post-positivism*, although both movements rose to prominence after the demise of positivism (a "modernist" position).

It is important to see that you slid from talking about belief to talking about truth—but these are not the same thing. We made the point in the first chapter (ably supported by Descartes, Locke, and Cromwell) that some (perhaps many) of our beliefs are wrong—are *not* true. The American pragmatist Charles Sanders Peirce, like Dewey later on, defined a belief as "that upon which a person is prepared to act," and of course if you believe X then you accept it as being true. (A man might believe that his salary check was automatically deposited in his bank account today by his employer; it would be strange to say that he believed this but was not prepared to act on it if the occasion demanded, or that he believed it but also held it not to be true—we would find the latter to be incoherent! In reality, of course, it does not follow from the fact that he believes this, that the belief is true or that it is false; it might be true, but it also could be the case that the salary was not deposited on time—the check might be "in the mail"!)

It is a confusion—and a pernicious one—to say that because a person believes X, and another doesn't, that X is both true and not true, or, relatedly, to say that there are "multiple (incompatible) realities." A few centuries ago, some people believed that the earth was round, whereas others believed it was flat. It was not possible for both views to be right. It *matters* what view was (or is) correct (especially for passengers in a boat or airplane). What is true is that some people *believe* X while others do not; the believers act accordingly and treat X as true while the others treat it as being false.

There certainly can be—and often are—multiple incompatible *beliefs* (who ever doubted it?). In 1492 many people believed the earth was flat, whereas Columbus and a few others believed it to be spherical; it is hard to credit that the earth really was *both* flat and spherical in 1492. When Columbus returned from his journey of exploration, many people changed their minds about the shape of the earth, but the shape itself did not change! The earth was (roughly) spherical in 1492, just as it is spherical now and just as it was spherical in 1392. Beliefs changed, not the actual shape of the earth. (And because the beliefs of many people changed, the way they were prepared to act also changed.)

This leads to another important point, one that is often misunderstood about postpositivists. Sometimes they are depicted as seeking "absolute truth," and this can be quite misleading. They will strive to form beliefs that are true (would they strive to form beliefs that are false?), but the matters about which they inquire will depend upon the precise problems with which they are dealing. Sometimes the issue might be *whether or not X is true*, in which case postpositivists will try to discover the truth about this ("Is the earth really spherical or flat?"). But on some other occasions what might be at stake is *whether some individual or group believes X to be true*, and postpositivists will then seek to discover the truth about this (i.e., they will pursue the issue of whether it is true that the members of this group believe X), which can be investigated independently of whether X actually is true or not. (Thus, "Do certain people believe the earth to be flat?" can be investigated by questioning or observing those people; the shape of the earth is not the issue; rather, it is their beliefs about the shape.)

Because in general humans act on their beliefs, that is, upon what they *suppose* to be true, it is often the case that researchers will be occupied with determining (truly) what these motivating beliefs are. (Columbus believed the Earth was spherical and therefore was prepared to act—to set sail out into the Atlantic Ocean; the point is that he would have acted the same way even if the Earth had turned out to be flat—for he believed it to be spherical!) Getting at the roots of human action, and the relation between thought and action, is a difficult enough task without complexifying the whole business by using misleading or confused ways of talking about the nature of human beliefs. Because people sometimes strongly believe or imagine the world to be a certain way, it has become colloquial to refer to "their" realities, almost in tacit recognition that these "realities" are particular to those individuals or groups. And, in some cases, their experiences and actions may be very much bounded by these "realities" that they accept. Although this is true in a cultural or psychological sense, these "realities" still bounce up against the same world inhabited by other people (with their own different beliefs about reality). What scientific research seeks, on the post-positivistic account, is a way to establish procedures and criteria that can support commonly adjudicated truth claims that do not depend solely on those subjectively experienced or believed "realities."

Three other points need to be made to forestall misunderstandings. First, it is common for all of us to talk rather loosely about things, or states-of-affairs, being true; we were guilty of this ourselves when we wrote of "X being true." But, technically, things just *are* (or perhaps, are *not*). A table is neither true nor false, for it simply is an object. The earth's shape is just a shape. And a state-of-affairs either exists or doesn't exist such that Val's computer is on the table. The predicates "true" and "false" apply only to *statements* or *propositions* about things or states-of-affairs; the statements that "Val's computer is on the table" or "the Earth is spherical in shape" or "there is a table over there" can be true or false (depending on what the particular states-of-affairs happen to be). In short, when we speak of the aim of research being the discovery of the truth about situations, we mean the discovery or formulation of true statements or theories about those situations (for a theory can be considered as simply a collection—perhaps a complex collection—of propositions).

Second, it should by now be obvious that we cannot always tell if a statement or theory or description of, or about, a situation or area of interest is true; but this does not mean that there is no truth of the matter in such a context (in the sense of "no true statements can be formulated here"). Different individuals might hold different sets of beliefs about such a situation, and some or perhaps even all of these beliefs might be true—but if we cannot tell if they are true, then we simply cannot tell! This does not mean it is useless to hold the view that there is a truth (or set of truths) about this situation. Popper and others, it will be recalled from chapter 1, held that belief in truth (or, more accurately, belief that there are some true statements that in principle could be put forward here) is a *regulative ideal*. It is a belief that drives our research efforts and makes us strive to adequately test our hypotheses and to detect errors. If we did not believe that truth can be found, in the sense explained above, why would we bother to carry out inquiries? If any old beliefs would suffice, we needn't bother to go to the trouble to do research—and often it is considerable trouble! But in fact we do attempt to carry out "competent inquiries," as Dewey put it, because in general we value the formulation of true rather than false beliefs, and we strive to achieve this goal.

Finally, again somewhat sloppily, we all sometimes speak of "the truth" as if there were only *one* truth to be discovered about any problem or situation. But of course there are *many* truths, even about the most mundane situations, and these truths are not conflicting or incompatible (even here, however, this does not mean that anything at all can be true, or that there is no way of testing for truth). It is true that one of the coauthors of this volume was born in Australia, that he was born shortly before the Second World War, and that he was born before his sister (these things are not true of the other author). It might be true of a particular classroom at a particular stage in a lesson that the teacher was challenging a student, that he was concerned about her progress, and that he believed she had not done her homework. The task for a researcher, very often, is to determine *which* of the many true statements that can be made about a situation are relevant (not to mention, of course, that the researcher also has to determine as far as is possible what statements *are* true about it). Relevance is determined with respect to the problem or issue that is being investigated.

Educational theorists such as Elliot Eisner sometimes criticize science for being one-dimensional. Unlike a work of art, a piece of science gives a very limited account of a situation and does not attempt to capture the richness, the complex reality, of situations such as those that occur in classrooms. The response to this point is that it is *not* a criticism! The point is that there is literally an infinite number of true propositions that could be formulated about any given situation, so it is not possible to state them all. Science does not attempt to describe the *total reality* (i.e., *all* the truths) about, say, a classroom; rather, it seeks to develop *relevant* true statements—ones that can serve to explain the situation that is of concern or that describe the causal relationships that are the focus of interest.

An example more closely related to educational and psychological research comes from a *Frontline* television documentary, "Divided Memories," that reported on work being done on so-called recovered memories of events from childhood or infancy. The program included many graphic and emotional scenes, for the director and camera operator had been granted access to groups in which people were receiving treatment for a variety of problems that—at least in the diagnosis of the therapists involved—could have their origins traced back to events in childhood, the memories of which were so painful that they had been repressed. The film shows some of the members of the various groups "recovering" these memories—a process that is almost as intense and painful for the viewer as it was for the individuals concerned.

One particularly striking segment showed a woman, who had evidently been troubled much of her adult life, recovering the memory of an extremely traumatic event from the start of her life—an event that seemingly had affected her adversely down through the years. She was in a trancelike condition and was sweating and appeared panic-stricken, as she recalled that—as a fertilized ovum—she had been trapped in her mother's fallopian tube for a short period. This recollection turned out to be cathartic for her, and the validity of the memory was enthusiastically endorsed by the therapist and the other members of the therapy group in front of whom it had been recovered.

A number of points can be made about this case. First, there seems to be little doubt that the woman involved, plus her fellow group members, plus the therapist, all *believed* that as an ovum she had been trapped in the fallopian tube; that is, they accepted this as a true state-of-affairs (technically, they accepted as true a proposition roughly along these lines: "When she was an ovum, she was trapped, and now she has correctly remembered this traumatic incident"). This woman's "recollection" might have been as real and vivid to her as any of her recollections of important events in her recent past. Second, because she—and they—believed, and accepted it as true, it influenced their subsequent behavior; the members of the group, and the therapist, were overjoyed that she had recovered this important memory while the woman herself felt relieved that at long last she had identified the hidden trauma that had been affecting her throughout the course of her life. (The film did not document it, but we can guess that her life might have been transformed by this belief. Certainly Sigmund Freud's patients often had their symptoms relieved by "understanding" the long-hidden causes of their psychopathologies.)

Third, a researcher who was interested in studying the efficacy of various treatments might (truly) conclude that if a patient comes to hold certain beliefs, she can find relief. To study this phenomenon, and to come to a conclusion like this, the researcher is not committed to accepting the patient's belief as true. It was the belief—the *acceptance* of the belief as being true—that produced the effect, *not* the actual truth of the belief. (This is a well-known phenomenon in educational psychology; for example, a student who believes she is poor at math will often perform poorly, whether or not she is *actually* poor at math. This is sometimes referred to as a self-fulfilling prophecy. Incorrect attributions of this kind are common in the classroom, and teachers need to be on guard against instilling them.) One of the therapists shown in the documentary actually stated something like this: "The patient believes this, and it was therapeutic. Who am I to question it? It was true for the patient, hence it must be true." The first part of this statement is true; the last part of it, however, is simply a confusion—it should be clear that the fact that a person holds a belief, even strongly or vehemently, is not evidence that the belief is actually true, and the case is not strengthened by the fact that the belief is held very strongly or that holding the belief had beneficial consequences for the person. (A faulty belief surely can have beneficial consequences for the individual holding it, but of course faulty beliefs also often can be harmful—as the example of false attribution of poor mathematical talent illustrates.)

Fourth, if a researcher is interested not in the *holding* of the belief but in the *truth* of the belief itself, the inquiry takes a different turn. We have good reason to think that individuals cannot recover memories of events that occurred when they were very young—and certainly not when they were at the single-cell stage of development—for the neurological apparatus required to form and retain memories was not present then, and neither was language! In fact, the ovum that developed into this person might have been temporarily trapped in the fallopian tube those many years ago; that is, her belief might in fact be true, but it is difficult to imagine how she could *have a reasonable warrant for asserting this to be the case*. In other words, it is her *assertion* that is extremely problematic—it is seriously to be doubted that her "recollection" was a genuine one (whether or not the event actually took place, which at this stage seems to be quite unknowable). This of course opens up another interesting line of research: How can false memories arise—memories so vivid that the individual having them has no doubt that they are correct? (Psychologist Elizabeth Loftus, among others, has studied the processes by which false memories can be implanted in people and then later "recovered" and accepted as true; see, for example, Loftus 1996, and the articles in Rubin 1996. It turns out to be not at all difficult to influence individuals to "recall" that some fictitious event—an event that can be documented as not having happened to them—actually did happen.)

## OBJECTIVITY, SUBJECTIVITY, AND BIAS

*Question:* Is it not the case that, as well as holding a strong notion of truth, postpositivists must also be committed to a robust notion of objectivity? In terms of the previous example, you appear to be claiming that it is objectively true that a person cannot remember what happened when he or she was an ovum. What is the difference, if any, between objectivity and truth?

*Response:* Again this is an interesting and important series of questions! Let us add to the difficulties here: Is "subjective" the contrasting term or alternative to "objective," or is "biased"? Or, perhaps, do "biased" and "subjective" mean the same thing? It is common these days to come across the charge that all viewpoints are to some degree biased (gender biased, racially biased, etc.). This is wonderfully illustrated by the statement attributed (rightly or wrongly) to Marion Barry, the controversial mayor of Washington, D.C.: "The laws of this city are clearly racist. All laws are racist. The law of gravity is racist." The issues here, of course, are of great moment in educational research. To mention an example that will be discussed in more detail later, is the concept of IQ (intelligence quotient) inherently biased, in the sense that certain groups in our society have "the deck stacked against them" so that, on average, their members will score lower on IQ tests than will members of the majority white, middle-class group—simply for the reason that the tests that define and measure "intelligence" contain items that members of the majority culture are more likely to be familiar with? (This issue is often confounded with two other and certainly related issues, namely, [1] do our social structures, educational practices, and reward systems systematically discriminate against those who are labeled as having "low IQ"? and [2] do all students have the same opportunities to develop the skills and capacities that IQ tests measure, including the test-taking facility itself? These are issues of social injustice or bias, and as such will not be the focus of our discussion, vitally important though they are; our focus here is on the nature of bias in research and in the theories, concepts, and practices that are used by researchers.)

The term "bias" has its origin in the old game of lawn bowls. The balls in this game have a built-in weight that is slightly off center, and when they are bowled along the grass they will always travel in a curve; they do not run "true" but always veer away if they are aimed straight at the target ball. This suggests that a bias in a person is a deep-seated characteristic or attitude that always shapes how that individual will behave, and there is a suggestion that the bias is relatively immune from eradication, and that it is illegitimate (not warranted by evidence or argument) in the contexts in which it is operating. Thus, a mathematics professor might be biased against students who are football players, whether or not they have mathematical ability but simply because they are "jocks," or an employer might be biased against Jews or women irrespective of how well they perform their job. It is interesting to note that the scholars who argue against the possibility of objectivity, claiming instead that in an important sense all views are "subjective" and offering arguments that they believe support this view, are not favorably disposed toward outright *bias*, as we shall see shortly. Virtually all of us regard the term as labeling an extremely negative characteristic, and if we were to detect it in the work of a researcher we would not judge that work favorably! (How we can reliably detect biases, in our own work and that of others, is not of course a trivial matter, and we shall return to it a little later.)

To revisit the example of IQ, it seems clear that an intelligence test should be labeled as biased if it has a built-in element that will systematically turn it away from the "true"—in this case, from giving a measure of "intelligence" rather than some other factor such as class or ethnicity or gender. And there seems to be solid historical evidence, dating right back to the origin of such tests in the work of

Binet and Simon and others in the years around the birth of the twentieth century, that the items used in these tests were, in large part, drawn from a stock of knowledge that was much more accessible to some groups in society than to others. (Binet and Simon, for example, "normed" their famous test on middle-class children in Paris and not on children living in slums or in the country; see the short but well-balanced discussion in Miller and Buckhout 1973, chap. 11.) In more recent times, and especially in the United States, IQ tests were charged with being "culturally biased" in that children not from the dominant middle class and largely white culture would not be able successfully to answer many of the items. This led, in the 1960s and 1970s, to the development of tests to illustrate this point, tests based on the experience of black children and on which middle-class whites performed extremely poorly. The following is an item from one such test:

> Tell what is being said in these sentences: "Did you check Adam's hog? The dude had a white on white in white with white. Ain't he foul. I talk to the cat but he was just too cool, he tried to high-sign me." (Miller and Buckhout 1973, 186)

Some postmodernist writers treat the bias that was found to exist in standard IQ tests as showing that the "modernist" or natural-science (or what we are calling the postpositivistic) position is inherently flawed (see essays in Kincheloe, Steinberg, and Gresson 1997). But it seems relevant to note that members of the educational testing community took the possibility of culture bias seriously and attempted to remedy this in their work, thus illustrating the point made above, that biased research is pretty universally regarded as *poor* research. (The history of testing, from Binet on, can be interpreted as being the history of attempts to improve tests and tease out their valid from their invalid uses; in other words, this history represents—to the postpositivist—the process by which fallible researchers, on the whole, try to benefit from their errors and improve their work, including making the effort to detect and eradicate bias. But it is also clear that, like *any* line of work, the "testing movement" is based on assumptions, and these certainly are not immune from criticism. To the postpositivist, as we have stressed, *nothing* is immune from criticism! A researcher in this tradition would not necessarily be biased—just insensitive perhaps, or ignorant—if he or she originally included culturally unfair items in the test; however, the researcher might well deserve to be identified as biased if he or she did nothing to address the situation after a critic had pointed it out.)

To return to the previous question, which asked about the link between objectivity and truth, it seems clear that these two terms are often used as if they were synonyms (an "objective opinion" is often thought to be one that is "true"), but sometimes they are coupled together for emphasis, a viewpoint commonly being referred to as "objectively true." All this seems to be a mistake. The fact is, objectivity does not *guarantee* that a belief or viewpoint is true (as we have stressed throughout, *nothing* can guarantee this). Consider one of the examples we mentioned very briefly earlier in this chapter. In the decades around the 1940s and 1950s biologists believed that the number of chromosomes in normal human cells was forty-eight. This view was not biased, and it was not subjective—it was held universally (or nearly so) by biologists, on the basis of objective evidence, that is, on the basis of evidence that was publicly available for inspection and that had been scrutinized by the relevant professional community and probably even had been "replicated" in several different laboratories. (The view that there were forty-eight chromosomes was not the quirky opinion of one or two individuals.) Nevertheless, this view turned out to be false. It is crucial to note, however, that the scientists (and the public) of the period had good reason to accept it (tentatively, as all the findings of science must be), for it was warranted by "objective" evidence, that is, the best evidence that was available at the time. One way to think about it is that "objectivity" is a label we apply to work, evidence, theories, and so forth, that meet certain criteria of excellence (those that come from what Dewey called "competent inquiries").

A lot remains to be said about objectivity and especially about its relationship to that most vexed of issues—the value neutrality of science. We shall turn to these complexities in the following chapter.

## REFERENCES

Elgin, Catherine. 1996. *Considered Judgment*. Princeton: Princeton University Press.

Gilligan, Carol. 1998. "Remembering Larry." *Journal of Moral Education* 27, no. 2: 125–140.

Kincheloe, J., S. Steinberg, and A. Greeson, eds. 1997. *Measured Lies: The Bell Curve Examined*. New York: St. Martin's/Griffin.

Loftus, E. 1996. *Eyewitness Testimony* Cambridge: Harvard University Press.

Lyotard, Jean-Francois. 1984. *The Postmodern Condition: A Report on Knowledge*. Manchester: Manchester University Press.

Miller, G., and R. Buckhout. 1973. *Psychology: The Science of Mental Life*. 2d ed. New York: Harper & Row.

Phillips, D. C. 1987. *Philosophy, Science, and Social Inquiry*. Oxford: Pergamon.

Phillips, D. C. 1997. "Coming to Grips with Radical Social Constructivisms." *Science and Education* 6, no. 1–2: 85–104.

Phillips, D. C. 1998. "How, Why, What, When, and Where: Perspectives on Constructivism in Psychology and Education." *Issues in Education: Contributions from Educational Psychology* 3, no. 2: 151–194.

Popper, K. 1965. *Conjectures and Refutations*. New York: Basic.

Rubin, D., ed. 1996. *Remembering Our Past: Studies in Autobiographical Memory*. Cambridge: Cambridge University Press.

# 3

# Objectivity, Relativity, and Value Neutrality

Objectivity is of the essence of science, just as subjectivity is of the essence of art. Natural scientists are natural objectivists. . . . But it is harder to be scientific, hence objective, about human affairs than about nature. . . . This is why social science is so much more backward than natural science. It is also why we often mistake opinions for data, value judgments for descriptive statements, and prophecies for forecasts. Further, this is why it is so important, for the advancement of social studies, to identify and expose the subjectivist philosophies that compound the natural obstacles to the objectivist or realist approach to social facts.

Mario Bunge

This passage, from a recent work by the prolific philosopher Mario Bunge (Bunge 1996, 326), nicely captures the view of many postpositivists. But clearly there are many controversial issues lying in wait for us as we expand on the ideas he touches upon above; we shall proceed as we did in the previous chapter, offering answers to the questions that can reasonably be asked.

*Question:* As you have depicted it, postpositivism is greatly concerned about the (postmodern?) skepticism that has arisen in recent years about the concept of truth and about objectivity in inquiry, especially in education and social science research generally (see, for example, Maxwell 1984). Your remarks (and those of Bunge) suggest that objectivity is not merely an important property of inquiry that can sometimes be jettisoned; rather, your view seems to be that objectivity is an essential aspect of competent inquiry, for without it inquiry hardly deserves that name and entirely loses its point. But why do some philosophers and researchers disagree? Is their discomfort with the concept of objectivity related to their concern that values always pervade inquiry? After all, the traditional view that they oppose holds that research in education and the social sciences is objective because it is value neutral. People who are incredulous about objectivity are necessarily incredulous about value neutrality. (You acknowledged earlier that inquirers always are situated culturally and historically and thus have the attendant attitudes, values, and biases.)

*Response:* There is a massive literature on the issue of whether or not the social sciences and educational research are, or should be, value neutral. More than four decades ago philosopher Richard Rudner already stated that the "mystical moment of dullness" had been reached (Rudner 1953, 231). It is not our main purpose to explain why an issue that, at first blush, appears to be so simple (and so dull) has for ages been the focus of attention, but it is arguable that there has been an extraordinary amount of loose thinking. Philosopher Antony Flew put it succinctly when he wrote that the opponents of value neutrality sometimes collapse important distinctions and "blunt" many vital subtleties (Flew 1985, 140). The same might be said for some of the proponents of the rival view!

Before we examine the arguments of those who attack the ideal of value neutrality as either impractical or mistaken, we need to make a few points about the relation between objectivity, relativity, and subjectivity. In the first place, there is deep-seated confusion between the adoption of different perspectives or frameworks by different inquirers (relativity), on the one hand, and a retreat into subjectivity on the other. For—as you recognized when you asked your question—every inquirer *must* adopt a framework or perspective or point of view. It is a truism that, given this framework or perspective, he or she may see phenomena differently from the way other investigators see them. But it does not follow from this that there is no fact of the matter or that "anything goes"—relativity of perspective does not *necessarily* lead to subjectivity, and relativity does not always warrant the charge of being biased. (See Eisner 1979, 214, for an example of this confusion in the educational literature.)

A spatial analogy might help clarify this point. If Denis were to stand in a room, against the wall opposite the only door to the room, and if Nick were to stand in the doorway, it is true that they would see the room differently. Denis would see the bookcase on the left wall, and Nick would see it on the right. Which view is the correct one? Clearly, the answer is: both. There is relativity of perspective here, but there is no subjectivity; and further, even though there is relativity there also can be objectivity. (Putnam 1981, 18–20, makes the same point using a different example.) To check that both answers about the bookcase are (objectively) correct, they could change places—Nick could look at the room from Denis's (previous) perspective, and Denis could look at it from Nick's. It is possible, of course, that one of them could have made a mistake. Denis might have gotten left and right muddled, and thus might have said, from his vantage point against the wall, that the bookcase was on the left when it wasn't; and Nick would then notice the mistake when they changed places. But this is a matter on which they could eventually reach agreement. It should be clear that in this example the relativity of Denis's and Nick's perspectives does not indicate that either of them is biased. (Another way to put it is that they had different frames of reference, and having a frame of reference is not the same as being biased.) Similarly, if Nick were to analyze a classroom incident from a Marxist perspective, and Denis from a Freudian one, this relativity of perspective would not indicate that either of them is biased—one or other of them might be, but this relativity does not establish it. (An economist and a sociologist both might study—from the perspective of their respective disciplines—the effects of a slump in the stockmarket; does the fact that they both have a perspective imply that they are biased?)

There is often a simple way to avoid the problems that arise when different inquirers have different perspectives (different theoretical frameworks, for example: the relativistic terms can be omitted and replaced by more objective language. To stay with the case of the room with the bookcase, it is possible to describe the room in such a way that the terms that are potential sources of confusion—"left" and "right"—are not used: "The bookcase is on the wall that is between the wall with the door and the wall with the window; and the bookcase is opposite the wall bearing the photograph of Karl Popper." A similar strategy can sometimes be used when there is a value-related difference (see Schrag 1989); for example, two classroom researchers with different values about gender equity and related matters might disagree about whether or not a particular teacher discriminates against girls in his class. They both see that he treats the boys differently but disagree that this is discrimination. Perhaps they could prevent their dispute from bogging down in a welter of value-laden terminology, and make more headway, by talking in the following way: "The teacher asked seventy-two questions during this class period, and, of these, he called upon boys to give answers to sixty-three; furthermore, he complimented boys on their answers six times as often as he complimented girls." This formulation has the advantage of clearly opening up the relevant issue in a very precise way, namely, the issue of why it is that the boys were called on far more frequently than the girls, and why they were praised so lavishly in comparison. (Of course there might also be more subtle indications of bias.) There is even a chance here that both researchers will come to agree that the teacher has no justification for his behavior and so must be biased (although, of course, it is possible that they might discover some explanation that makes him look more reasonable—it might be a large class made up largely of boys, or the girls might have transferred from another class in which they had already covered the material in this lesson, but for the boys the material was new and difficult).

One point needs to be stressed in order to forestall a misunderstanding of the position being advanced here. Clearly it will not always be the case that a researcher's perspective will be unproblematic and easily "translatable" into neutral or objective terminology. Sometimes the perspective will be so distorted by his or her values or ideological assumptions, and so on, that the charge of bias will be well-founded. Cases of the following kind come to mind, in which the value position that was held was akin to a broad ideology that influenced not only many of the researcher's beliefs and attitudes but also the experimental procedures that were adopted (and not adopted); the example is documented by Stephen J. Gould (Gould 1981, chap. 3). Paul Broca, the nineteenth-century French medical researcher, had measured the cranial capacity of skulls of men and women of different races. He believed that brain size was related to intelligence and that because white men were superior in intelligence they would have larger brains than women and males of other ethnic groups. When Broca came across white males whose brain size was too small, he corrected for such factors as body size and age. But he did not make similar corrections for data coming from women or from men of other ethnicities. It seems clear that Broca had allowed his values to intrude into his work in such a way that the objectivity of his science was destroyed. In short, Broca was biased (and, significantly, in this case at least, he also did poor science).

## CRITIQUES OF THE VALUE NEUTRALITY OF RESEARCH

*Question:* So far you have discussed some points about subjectivity. You made the point that although researchers always have a framework or perspective, this need not necessarily compromise their objectivity. But what about the main concern: what are the flaws that exist in the arguments (or metanarratives, to use Lyotard's expression) offered by those who argue that value neutrality is never attainable in the social sciences and educational research?

*Response:* A number of different lines of argument have been developed, each of which we shall examine in turn, labeling them argument A to argument F. In the course of our discussion we shall from time to time use the example of IQ testing, which nicely illustrates many of the points at stake. (This discussion is indebted to some points made in Phillips 1992, chap. 10.)

### Argument A

One clearly inadequate argument runs as follows: "Educational researchers study the prominent aspects of human and social phenomena as these pertain to schooling and learning. It is simply a fact that societies, and the individuals who belong to them—including teachers and others involved in the educational enterprise—place value on certain things. Thus the researcher—depending upon his or her specific interests—may want to *study values*, and the process of valuation. Hence values must enter into educational research." Unfortunately for this argument, from the fact that values are sometimes the objects of study in the social sciences and educational research, it does not follow that values influence the concepts or the procedures that are used in the course of such inquiries. It is this latter issue, and not the former, that has been at stake in the prolonged debates over value neutrality in research. (In other words, this particular argument or metanarrative does not show that it is impossible for a researcher to study, in an objective way, such things as the values that are held by Amish parents about the education of their children.)

## Argument B

Another argument against value neutrality fares no better: "It is clear that many researchers have allowed their racist or sexist attitudes to bias their work, and there are many cases in which economic or ideological interests have swayed a researcher—such as when a scientist working for a tobacco company allows his employment situation to influence the sorts of research designs that are used and the nature of the data that are collected, or when an educational researcher interprets data in a way that denigrates children from a minority culture (as is sometimes the case when test scores are interpreted). A classic case in the literature concerns T. D. Lysenko in the Soviet Union of Stalin's time, who allowed his Communist values (or his desire for personal power and advancement) to influence his views on genetics, with disastrous repercussions. Mendelian genetics was suppressed for a period, and a faulty approach based on Lamarckian principles was adopted in Russian agricultural plant breeding programs. Some Mendelians were purged and exiled to Siberia where they died (Zirkle 1959; Shipman 1988, 132–133). In short, cases like this demonstrate that values do influence the work of scientists!

Unfortunately, again, this argument is beside the point. It is clear that humans are not angels; they do many things that are not worthy of emulation (together with what is probably a smaller number of things that are). The fact that some athletes take steroids does not establish steroid use as a part of the fabric of sport. The fact that—as Woody Allen has pointed out—some of our politicians are both incompetent and corrupt (and often on the same day) does not establish that politicians have to be that way. Similarly, the fact that some scientists allow biases to intrude into their work does not establish either that this has to be the case or that *the rules or criteria of the scientific enterprise (the "cognitive values" as some call them) endorse the entry of such biases.* Broca, for example, would be universally condemned these days for doing science that was flawed, and few if any scientists would praise his practice of biasing the evidence—which goes some way to showing that the ideal of value-free science is widely endorsed. And the awful consequences of Lysenko's work actually illustrate the virtue of the ideal of value neutrality—his work was disastrous simply because he *did* allow his political values to intrude into his science. Finally, since it was typically later science that revealed such biases, it seems contradictory to claim that all science is biased.

*Question:* At this point one can hear the opponents of value neutrality heaving a sigh of relief: "You have conceded the case," they will say, "for here you have explicitly stated that there *is* an *ideal*—it is patently obvious that acceptance of the principle that science should be value-free is itself the acceptance of a value!"

*Response:* This is a good argument; the ideal of value-free inquiry is what we will later call an *internal* or *cognitive* value. But before we clarify this, let us examine two further and closely related arguments that are often put forward to show that value-free social science is not possible. We shall state them both before offering comments.

## Argument C

There is a relatively more subtle and powerful metanarrative against the possibility of value neutrality that has a number of interesting variants. The core argument (favored by some of the social constructivists we referred to earlier) runs as follows: "Some value orientations are so embedded in our modes of thought as to be unconsciously held by all scientists, or, more precisely, by all those working within the same sociohistorical context. This situation has arisen because all inquiries have to make use of categories and concepts, principles, rules of evidence, and so forth; and these things will by necessity have been developed so as to reflect the interests of the most powerful groups in society. Over time these particular ways of conceptualizing the world, and inquiry, will become embedded. To give just one example, some scholars in the Marxist tradition have suggested that the interests and values of Western capitalism have permeated the social sciences and educational research in this way." (See Moten 1990 for a similar criticism made by an Islamic scholar.)

## Argument D

Some feminist scholars would agree with the general point made above; their version of the metanarrative might run as follows: "Feminist philosopher Sandra Harding argues that 'the most fundamental categories of scientific thought are male biased' (Harding 1987, 290), a consequence of male power and the resultant domination over modes of inquiry for long periods of time. It is important to note here that Harding is not simply claiming that the issues pursued in many branches of science reflect male interests, a claim that is entirely credible, and the recognition of which promises to redress many inequities in fields such as education and medicine; she is going further and is claiming that the categories or conceptual tools of science are male biased."

What is to be made of these related lines of argument? It is important to note that a two-pronged case needs to be presented if the general charge against value neutrality made in these two metanarratives is to be upheld. In the first place, it needs to be established (presumably by some sort of historical study) that Western capitalists or white males have in fact been dominant in the requisite way and have had the capacity and the opportunity to insert their values into social science and education research (a case that is probably relatively easy to make). But, second, it needs to be shown—this time by a much more difficult argument—that the white male or Western capitalist categories or principles that have been introduced in this way (such things as the principle of objectivity, and the view that attainment of true belief is a regulative ideal, for example) are in some sense biased. (Some may be, but are all of them?) That is, every one of these categories or principles has to be shown to subvert or misdirect inquiry; but it is worth pointing out that this is an impossible charge to substantiate if inquiry necessarily is always subverted. Bias or subversion or misdirection are concepts that only have application if it is possible to have inquiry that is unbiased, unsubverted, unmisdirected—for, as we saw earlier, bias is defined as departure from the straight and narrow, from the "true." But in a world in which there is no true, the notion of bias is drained of content; the accusation of bias against Broca or Lysenko, for example, loses its sting if all inquiry necessarily is biased. (Postpositivists would insist that it is vital to maintain our ability to detect and eradicate biases such as theirs.) Sandra Harding's position is interesting but complex; we shall examine it in more detail near the end of the chapter.

*Question:* In the literature critical of the possibility of value neutrality in educational research, other arguments (or metanarratives) often appear. In particular, it has been pointed out that social scientists have to select problems to pursue, and they also have to criticize and make evaluations of each other's work; surely both of these processes involve values?

*Response:* In addressing these points, we need to introduce several overlooked distinctions that also will throw light on the earlier point about value neutrality itself being a value, an internal value, in science. But first, the two arguments to which you refer in your last remark need to be spelled out more fully.

### Argument E

One of the positions you referred to runs as follows: "There are infinitely many problems that a scientist can decide to examine, from which he or she manages to select a small number to pursue. So clearly the scientist has some decision criteria, and these often—if not always—reflect that particular scientist's sexist or cultural or other biases, or judgments about what is valuable or socially important. Such value decisions are reinforced by governmental or other funding agencies, which have clear-cut value priorities; for example, educational research projects that are regarded as trivial or subversive or politically disadvantageous are not regularly funded. In other words, values necessarily enter the social sciences and educational research in this way."

## Argument F

The other argument can take various forms. One common version, put forward by both Michael Scriven (Scriven 1974) and Richard Rudner (Rudner 1953), is quite straightforward: "The researcher, in his or her role as a researcher, has to judge or evaluate hypotheses, theories, data, and so forth (Rescher 1976, lists seven broad areas in which scientists have to make such judgments); it is clear that evaluation requires values. Hence, in order for the researcher to carry on with business, values must occupy a place within social science and education research." (See also Zecha 1992.)

## INTERNAL, EPISTEMICALLY RELEVANT VALUES—AND THEIR OPPOSITE

*Question:* Both argument E and argument F seem correct. Don't they establish that values must be present in research?

*Response:* Both of these arguments, and the earlier point about the principle of value neutrality itself being a value, can be addressed by drawing a pair of related distinctions, first, between *external or extrascientific* values and *internal or intrascientific or cognitive* values and, second, between *epistemologically relevant* and *epistemologically irrelevant* values.

The first of these distinctions is conveniently introduced via an analogy (sports experts will not want to take this too seriously). Historically, the game of baseball has undergone a number of changes in its rules or practices. Some of these were imposed from "outside," for example, by team owners who were anxious to increase the appeal of the game to paying "customers" (arguably the introduction of a "designated hitter" was one of these). Such changes served external values, usually simply the making of a profit (there was no absolutely compelling reason "internal" to the game, for example, for making this particular change). But other changes have been made to further the game *as a game*; these have furthered the internal values of the game. And, of course, some changes presumably have done both—the rule against "roughing the quarterback" in American football not only protects an expensive investment made by the team owner in a player who is often a great drawing card with the members of the public, but it also allows the quarterback more opportunity to display his skill without undue fear of being seriously injured. Sometimes, then, the external values might enhance the internal workings of the game; sometimes they do not much affect the quality of the game itself (the sanctions imposed against disorderly or immoral conduct off the field, for example). Sometimes they might even work against the internal values and thus make the game in some respects less than it was.

Similar points can be made about research. The one crucial for our purposes, however, is that although extra scientific values might determine *what* the scientist will study, this does not mean that those very same values necessarily must internally influence *how* it is studied—and it is this latter issue that is the key one at stake in the dispute over the value neutrality of research (Nagel 1961, 486–487, makes a similar point). Thus, Joe Dromedary might receive an external research grant from an antismoking group to study the influence of "passive smoke" on the family members of smokers. Although it is not an ideal situation that such outside agents can select, in effect, what Joe studies, it is probably an inevitable fact of life in the modern world, given the economic realities of the costs of research. And it is not a complete tragedy, for the (internal) scientific quality of Joe Dromedary's work on this topic need not be influenced by the source of his funding. Clearly it would become tragic if external funding agents or his own extrascientific values (perhaps he is a smoker himself!) influenced his work so that he was prepared to falsify data or compromise the research design in order to protect these external interests. (It goes almost without saying that the internal values of science forbid falsifying data or compromising research designs to further ideological or other external ends.)

All this can be summarized in the form of an aphorism: *It is still possible for a field of research that is externally influenced by values to operate internally in a relatively objective manner (indeed it is crucial for the scientific enterprise that it does so), but a field whose internal workings are significantly influenced by external values has been seduced.* A classic example of such seduction is the aforementioned Lysenko, who threw his weight against Mendelian genetics and in support of Lamarckian heredity (which had been largely discredited by years of competent scientific research), not on the basis of any reputable scientific considerations but because Lamarck was easier to reconcile with the principles of Communism and was therefore more likely to find favor with Stalin (which it did). This case illustrates the point that a field of research that has been internally seduced by external values may well face disaster, for on the whole it will produce poor science. Internal to any field of science, decisions have to be made according to the relevant rules and criteria pertinent to the field itself; and if they are not, they are likely to be scientifically poor decisions. These rules do not require scientific research or the people who carry it out to be value-free; rather, it is a matter of appreciating any clash that may exist between some of the values that scientists hold as individuals and the internal or cognitive values involved in the scientific enterprise.

The second and perhaps more fundamental distinction exists between *epistemically relevant* and *epistemically irrelevant* values. Lysenko's political values (or his desire for personal fame or advancement) led to disaster when allowed to interfere internally in genetics because those values were epistemically irrelevant. That is, given that the intellectual aim of genetics is to produce well-warranted knowledge of genetic phenomena (i.e., knowledge of inheritance, of the factors that affect the expression of the genes in the phenotype, of the biochemical structure of genes, and so forth), then the relevant criteria to be used within genetics are the ones that have been settled upon, over extended periods of time and by researchers working in that and similar fields, as criteria that are likely to further this epistemic aim. Political values are not relevant—and have never been shown to be relevant—to the field's epistemological ambitions. (There are, of course, several interesting issues relating to the notion of "epistemic relevance" that need to be pursued but cannot be discussed here; and of course the judgment about what *is* epistemically relevant or irrelevant is itself—like *all* judgments—potentially a fallible one! Here again, accountability within a research community to which such judgments need to be justified is one of the key—if imperfect—safeguards that we can have.)

The two distinctions that we have introduced can be used to criticize metanarrative F. When refereeing a research paper for a journal, for example, which is a clear case of evaluation within science, a reader certainly draws upon values; but in the main they are supposed to be intrascientific and epistemologically relevant values. (The "in the main" is necessary because "aesthetic" and "rhetorical" criteria are also used as subsidiary considerations; for example, the paper's organization might be difficult to follow or the writing awkward and ungrammatical.) As we both know from personal experience, editorial boards require that referees state reasons for their recommendations, especially when it is suggested that the paper be rejected; we find it hard to imagine any editors of scholarly journals who would be satisfied with reasons based entirely on a referee's own external value prejudices. Instead, it is expected that the evaluator will point to such epistemically relevant things as fallacies in the reasoning, errors in the data analysis, or flaws in the design of the study that is being reported. Furthermore, the word of a single referee is not trusted on these matters; most journals consult at least three people for each paper.

It should be clear that our argument has conceded *part* of the case of those who argue that research cannot, and should not, be value neutral. But it is important to note which part of this case we have conceded! We have placed great emphasis on the fact that the values that do, and must, play a role within research are restricted to the category of epistemically relevant, internal values—values like dedication to the pursuit of truth, openness to counter evidence, receptiveness to criticism, accuracy of measurements and observations, honesty and openness in reporting results, and the like. These values foster the epistemic concerns of science as an enterprise that produces competent warrants for knowledge claims. In short, these relevant values are constitutive of scientific inquiry; that is, without them scientific inquiry loses its point. Nobody, to our knowledge, has ever denied that such values exist or has suggested that scientific inquiry can proceed without them. Philosopher Ernan McMullin has asserted, correctly, that science is value laden in the sense "that there are certain characteristic epistemic values which are integral to the entire process of assessment in science" (McMullin 1983, 6). Gerhard Zecha points out that Max Weber and many others have held similar views (Zecha 1992, 155). Philosopher of science Larry Laudan has also written of the central importance of what he called *cognitive values* in science (which are the same as those we call "internal values"):

> In this book . . . I have nothing to say about ethical values as such, for they are manifestly not the predominant values in the scientific enterprise. Not that ethics plays no role in scence. . . . But that importance fades into insignificance when compared to the ubiquitous role of cognitive values. (Laudan 1984, xii)

That role, Laudan says, is the "shaping of scientific rationality."

The classic dispute about values—the dispute that has fired controversies for more than a century—is about whether or not external, nonepistemically relevant values (e.g., political or religious values, or values relating to one's position of power in society or to one's economic interests) legitimately and perhaps necessarily play a role in scientific research. In common with most if not all postpositivists we have made no concessions on this point but have maintained that a research field has been seduced if it allows such values to intrude internally. Research must be free of serious contamination by such epistemically irrelevant, external values. (The pressing issue of how we can best detect and expunge such values is one to which we shall return shortly; we also discuss Sandra Harding's interesting suggestion about this matter.)

The position that has been argued here can be strengthened by suggesting that, in general, if not in all cases, the internal and cognitively or epistemically relevant values should be regarded as not being moral or ethical values—at least in the internal contexts in which they legitimately appear (Laudan too seems to be suggesting this in the quotation above). To outsiders, the researcher who has knowingly fudged his or her data (as did Sir Cyril Burt in his research on the intelligence of twins who were reared apart; see Hearnshaw 1979) may be morally reprehensible, but within science the sin is a *scientific* one. The researcher is guilty of having contravened the epistemically relevant rules of science and in so doing has done poor science. Similarly, the researcher who opens his or her work to strong criticism from peers is not morally good but is a *good researcher* and simply is doing what is required of all researchers if the scientific enterprise is to have any chance of achieving its epistemic goals. The two contexts—inside science and the outside world—are of course likely to run together in most minds, for scientists inhabit both worlds and cannot completely shed their outside values when they enter the laboratory; what they can do, however, is to take precautions that their outside values do not distort the research that they carry out.

## AN EXAMPLE: THE HISTORY OF IQ TESTING

*Question:* This has been a complex case—necessarily so, given your point that much of the literature is not careful enough in making crucial distinctions. Can you give a pithy summary and provide a detailed example relevant to educational research?

*Response:* Clearly researchers in education and the social sciences have occasionally allowed their personal political or religious or social values to influence their work. The ideal of value-free scientific investigation is not refuted by this, for the ideal does not endorse such influence. Of course, researchers can still hold their values, but their scientific decisions have to be warranted by relevant scientific considerations. Sometimes the questions they pursue in the course of their professional lives have been determined by the value preferences of funding agencies and the like; this is probably unavoidable so long as scientists require substantial research moneys to carry out their work. Although it is not ideal, it again does not lead to the subversion of the ideal of value-free science—so long as the sources of funding do not have improper influence over the internal or cognitive values of science and over how these values are applied in practice. The ideal of value-free scientific investigation boils down to this: The activities of science should be internally directed by the values—the so-called cognitive values—that are relevant to the aim of science to produce warranted knowledge; these activities should not be subverted by external and irrelevant values and biases.

The development of the IQ test, and the subsequent controversies surrounding it, can serve as an example to illustrate these points. (The history here is very rich and clearly cannot be treated adequately in the short space we have to devote to it.) Alfred Binet was the central figure in the development of the IQ test, although his name is often coupled with that of Simon. Binet was working during a time of heightened interest in human mental capacities and in the role of heredity in shaping them. The work of Charles Darwin's brilliant cousin, Francis Galton, had produced evidence for the heritability of some factors (he had studied how genius seems to run in families, for example); he had also started on the process of developing statistical techniques that might be useful in these kinds of studies and for throwing light on the distribution of individual differences in various capacities or characteristics. (Darwin's theory of evolution itself raised the issue of what factors in humans were adaptive factors that had been developed to high pitch by natural selection. Darwin had tried to avoid discussing human characteristics, for he abhorred controversies, but nearer the end of the century there were many individuals who were bolder. In the United States, William James believed that the human capacity to think was an adaptive feature acquired in the course of evolution, which at least raised the possibility that individuals might differ in the degree to which they possessed this capacity, although James did not pursue this matter.)

In the late nineteenth century there was no consensus in the scientific community about how to measure human intelligence, or about its nature or status. There was a broadly shared judgment—clearly one that Binet shared—that this was an interesting area for scientific study; this judgment arose internally in the relevant scientific community as a consequence of the scientific climate outlined above. There is no evidence to believe that Binet was biased or that he was lacking in objectivity, although—like all of us—he was constrained by what was available in the science of his day.

A number of external influences did come to play a role in the story, however. The French Ministry of Public Instruction became concerned that there might be many "subnormal" students in the public schools, whose education might be helped if they were identified and placed in special schools (a not uncommon policy issue in many countries around the world even today). A commission was set up to study the matter, on which Binet served. But he soon became disturbed that the commissioners were extremely vague and confused about what constituted "retardation" (i.e., they were relying on their own prejudices or hunches about retardation), and he set out to find more objective grounds on which to base their deliberations. Binet started a collaboration with Simon, a physician working in an asylum for "backward" children, whose concern seems to have been that many of his charges were incorrectly diagnosed and were not backward at all! Clearly, then, these two men had strong humanitarian values that drove their work in seeking an objective measurement of intelligence and retardation. But these values did not seem to interfere internally in the scientific decisions they reached. In brief, they chose a number of test items and tried them out in Paris schools, conducting interviews and testing sessions with many children and also talking with teachers. Items that did not distinguish between younger or older children were discarded, as were items that did not distinguish between students whom teachers agreed were average or severely backward. They produced the first version of their test in 1905 and a second version in 1908; they had a group of items that more than half of three-year-olds could get right, and so on up to the age of thirteen. If a child with the chronological age of six could only answer correctly the items that an average four-year-old could get right, then that child had a mental age of four and was judged as being retarded by two years. Binet did not believe that the test necessarily measured a fixed capacity in the children—he seems to have been aware of the dangers of reifying IQ (an appreciation unfortunately not always shared by later users of the test).

Judged in terms of the (internal) criteria of the science of the times, Binet and Simon had done a good piece of work, although at first it was more widely recognized and used outside France. But clearly it had flaws, and there was much room for improvement. The test provided a rich base on which later researchers could build in interesting—and sometimes controversial—ways. One tradition of researchers used statistical techniques to determine how many "psychological factors" were responsible for producing a student's score; one result of this tradition was the hypothesis that there was a general intellectual ability factor, "g," at work alongside a number of more specific abilities (spatial, for example). Other researchers, assuming that intelligence or general intellectual ability was heritable, attempted to show this by studying the intelligence of identical twins reared together versus those reared apart (the latter being quite a rare circumstance). The reasoning here was that as identical twins have precisely the same genetic makeup, the IQ of twins would be very close, even if they had been reared apart, and their IQs would be closer to each other's than they would be to the IQs of other family members or individuals with whom they had been brought up in the same environment. In Britain, Cyril Burt spent much of his life collecting the rare data on identical twins who had been separated shortly after birth and reared apart. These data were destroyed during a bombing raid on London during the Second World War; Burt at first tried to reconstruct them from memory but ended by inventing data, which came to light after he died. Clearly his actions contravened the internal values of science and he was universally condemned. (It is not entirely clear what his external motives were, if any; and there are some indications that he may have developed a mental disorder. See Hearnshaw 1979 for a detailed account of Burt's work.)

Nearer the present day, Arthur Jensen examined the impact of IQ on the lack of success of many remedial education programs, and his work embodied the suggestion that there are genetically determined racial differences in IQ (Jensen 1969). His long essay, and the rebuttals and commentaries, filled several issues of the *Harvard Educational Review*. A similar theme, meeting similar reactions, was developed a quarter of a century later in Herrnstein's and Murray's controversial book, *The Bell Curve* (1994), which argued that the United States was becoming stratified into classes defined largely in terms of IQ differences. These three researchers were accused of racism and of allowing their values to influence their work (i.e., they were accused of allowing their external values to internally influence their science), although they believed they were merely pushing their research into sensitive areas that nonetheless ought to be systematically investigated. "Sensitive" is probably something of an understatement—in both 1969 and 1994 feelings quickly reached the boiling point. Jensen's life was threatened and for a period he was accompanied everywhere by a bodyguard. Herrnstein and Murray have been accused of producing "hoodoo social science," of embodying in their work the ideals of "white supremacy," of fostering the "politics of fear and loathing," and of producing a book that is "intellectually worthless" (see essays in Kincheloe, Steinberg, and Greeson 1997). The reactions to Herrnstein and Murray's book are particularly pertinent to the analysis we have given of value neutrality; the critics move to and fro between pointing out (correctly) that the book is full of errors—that it is poor quality research—and stressing (correctly) the value-laden and politically partisan nature of the work, thus supporting our analysis that science which allows external values to intrude internally is likely to be very poor science. What some of these critics do not acknowledge, however, is that the work of Herrnstein and Murray can only deserve these criticisms if, indeed, it is *both desirable and possible for research to be free of these various defects*—only if, in fact, the ideal of value neutrality (in the sense of freedom from external interference in the internal and epistemically relevant operations of science) is accepted.

However, there is one aspect of the reactions to Herrnstein and Murray that seems more problematic when seen through postpositivistic eyes. Some critics seem to believe that the defects in Herrnstein and Murray indicate that there are fatal flaws in the scientific enterprise itself. As Kincheloe and Steinberg put it:

> Not only is *The Bell Curve* weak science marked by unreliable sources, the dismissal of problematic data, logical non sequiturs and misguided purposes, it emerges from a crumbling paradigm often deemed inadequate for the complex study of human intelligence. . . . Herrnstein and Murray perpetuate the myth of modern science that the universe is totally knowable and controllable. . . . The cognitive psychology they employ is the product of the Cartesian-Newtonian paradigm. (Kincheloe and Steinberg, in Kincheloe, Steinberg, and Gresson 1997, 27–28)

Certainly there is nothing in postpositivism, as we have been developing it, that assumes the universe is "totally knowable and controllable." But of course we do assume—along with all researchers of all stripes—*that it is worth making the attempt to know*. (After all, should we assume that some things are unknowable prior to making a serious attempt to reach understanding? To assume that things are unknowable spells the end to any inquiry. And how, of course, are we to establish that they are unknowable?) However, the criticism of Herrnstein and Murray quoted above, whether well-founded or not, raises a vitally important issue for the postpositivist: *How far can we go in studying human affairs (including educational phenomena) using the methods of natural science—using the so-called Cartesian-Newtonian paradigm?* This question is so important that it deserves—and will receive—a chapter of its own.

## THE DETECTION OF BIAS AND THE INTERNAL INFLUENCE OF EXTERNAL VALUES

*Question:* There is a lingering issue that must be resolved. Throughout, you have acknowledged that some researchers undoubtedly will be biased, and it is apparent that some researchers do allow "epistemically irrelevant" values or attitudes to intrude into their work, whether wittingly or not. You also indicated earlier in the discussion that it is not always easy to detect such illegitimate influences. What can we do to guard against them?

*Response:* Clearly, there is no absolutely foolproof way to insulate educational research against such things. Once again Karl Popper seems to have been on the right track. He asserted that we cannot expect researchers to become superhuman (or, more likely, less than human) by shedding or suppressing their interests, concerns, values, religious beliefs, and so forth. What protects science from intrusion by nonepistemically relevant values is the fact that science is organized as a communal activity, with a tradition of open inquiry and discussion, of replication, of *peer review*, and so forth. It is the openness of work to criticism that is the best (though not perfect) safeguard that we have that errors, assumptions, values, and biases will get rooted out and exposed to the light for discussion. Popper once imagined that Robinson Crusoe was a scientist, who, in the course of solitary work on his island, had reached the same results that our own science had produced in some field; in Popper's view this outcome would be quite accidental and miraculous. Why?

> For there is nobody but himself to check his results; nobody but himself to correct those prejudices which are the unavoidable consequence of his peculiar mental history; nobody to help him get rid of that strange blindness concerning the inherent possibilities of our own results which is a consequence of the fact that most of them are reached through comparatively irrelevant approaches. . . . it may be said that what we call "scientific objectivity" is not a product of the individual scientist's impartiality, but a product of the social or public character of scientific method; and the individual scientist's impartiality is, so far as it exists, not the source but rather the result of this socially or institutionally organized objectivity of science. (Popper 1945, 374)

It is interesting that recent work by feminist philosophers has also stressed the role played by the "epistemic community." But they tend to see it as a role that is even more important than the one Popper acknowledged. Thus, Lynn Hankinson Nelson (among others) argues the strong thesis that the "unit" or "agent" in epistemology is not the individual knower (who, she says, has usually been the focus in traditional foundationalist epistemologies); rather, it is the community:

> My arguments suggest that the collaborators, the consensus achievers, and in more general terms, the agents who generate knowledge are communities and subcommunities, not individuals. (Nelson 1993, 124)

Her point is that what is to count as evidence, as "competent" procedures, and so forth, are all matters that require communal assent. (We saw in chapter 1 that the work of Thomas S. Kuhn was crucial in bringing the role of the community to the fore in philosophy of science.)

Sandra Harding has developed a somewhat different line of thought, although she would not disagree with the points made above; rather, she would think they do not go far enough. She agrees that science should be objective, but her concern is that there are deep and therefore hidden sources of bias that are unlikely to be identified and eradicated if we rely solely on the mechanism of open criticism favored by the likes of Popper. As we mentioned earlier, she argues, for example, that there are deep male biases built into the very category systems used in science. Because these are widely taken for granted (within the predominantly male scientific community), they are unlikely to be challenged and removed, simply because they are not seen to be biases at all but have become part of the unquestioned cultural background against which contemporary science is practiced. She writes:

> The problem with the conventional conception of objectivity is not that it is too rigorous or too "objectifying," as some have argued, but that it is *not rigorous or objectifying enough*; it is too weak to accomplish even the goals for which it has been designed, let alone the more difficult projects called for by feminisms and other new social movements. (Harding 1996, 237)

Harding, then, wants to achieve what she calls "strong objectivity" that can grapple with these deep-seated sexist and other biases. This is to be done by developing what she calls "feminist standpoint epistemology," which sets out from the premise

> that in societies stratified by race, ethnicity, class, gender, sexuality, or some other such politics shaping the very structure of a society, the *activities* of those at the top both organize and set limits on what persons who perform such activities can understand about themselves and the world around them. (Harding 1996, 240)

It is only marginalized people at the bottom of the social ladder who can see certain things as problematic—as being values of the dominant group that have become so built-in that they are invisible to many at the top. The way to achieve strong objectivity, then, is to enfranchise the marginalized groups—to incorporate them as full members of the epistemic community.

Whether or not one agrees with Harding or regards the mechanism of open criticism advocated by Popper as being sufficient, it is clear that objectivity is both important and difficult to achieve. It remains the sine qua non of research, for without it, we don't have research at all! The present authors are not fully convinced that Harding has made her point about inherent male bias on epistemological grounds (some aspects of her "metanarrative" were discussed earlier in this chapter) but are convinced that her bottom line is incontestable: On grounds of social equity, at the very least, our knowledge-generating communities ought to become fully representative and open. They cannot be anything but stronger scientific communities if they are to be so.

# REFERENCES

Bunge, Mario. 1996. *Finding Philosophy in Social Science*. New Haven: Yale University Press.

Eisner, Elliot. 1979. *The Educational Imagination*. New York: Macmillan.

Flew, Antony. 1985. *Thinking about Social Thinking*. Oxford: Blackwell.

Gould, Stephen J. 1981. *The Mismeasure of Man*. New York: Norton.

Harding, Sandra. 1987. "The Instability of the Analytical Categories of Feminist Theory." In *Sex and Scientific Inquiry*. Edited by Sandra Harding and Jean O'Barr. Chicago: University of Chicago Press.

Harding, Sandra. 1996. "Rethinking Standpoint Epistemology: What Is 'Strong Objectivity'?" In *Feminism and Science*. Edited by Evelyn Fox Keller and Helen Longino. Oxford: Oxford University Press.

Hearnshaw, L. S. 1979. *Cyril Burt: Psychologist*. Ithaca, N.Y.: Cornell University Press.

Herrnstein, R., and C. Murray. 1994. *The Bell Curve: Intelligence and Class Structure in American Life*. New York: Free Press.

Jensen, A. 1969. "How Much Can We Boost IQ and Scholastic Achievement?" *Harvard Educational Review* 39: 1–123.

Kincheloe, J., S. Steinberg, and A. Greeson, eds. 1997. *Measured Lies: The Bell Curve Examined*. New York: St. Martin's/Griffin.

Laudan, Larry. 1984. *Science and Values*. Berkeley: University of California Press.

Maxwell, Nicholas. 1984. *From Knowledge to Wisdom*. New York: Blackwell.

McMullin, Ernan. 1983. "Values in Science." In *PSA 1982*. Edited by Peter Asquith and Thomas Nickles. Vol. 2. East Lansing, Mich.: Philosophy of Science Association.

Moten, Rashid. 1990. "Islamization of Knowledge: Methodology of Research in Political Science." *American Journal of Islamic Social Science* 7: 106–113.

Nagel, Ernest. 1961. *The Structure of Science*. London: Routledge.

Nelson, Lynn Hankinson. 1993. "Epistemological Communities." In *Feminist Epistemologies*. Edited by Linda Alcoff and Elizabeth Potter. New York: Routledge.

Phillips, D. C. 1992. *The Social Scientist's Bestiary*. Oxford: Pergamon.

Popper, K. [1945] 1985. "Against the Sociology of Knowledge." In *Popper Selections*. Edited by B. Magee. Princeton: Princeton University Press.

Putnam, Hilary. 1981. *Reason, Truth, and History*. Cambridge: Cambridge University Press.

Rescher, Nicholas. 1976. "The Role of Values in Social Science Research." In *Controversies and Decisions: The Social Sciences and Public Policy*. Edited by Charles Frankel. New York: Russell Sage Foundation.

Rudner, Richard. [1953] 1980. "The Scientist Qua Scientist Makes Value Judgments." In *Introductory Readings in Philosophy of Science*. Edited by E. D. Klemke, R. Hollinger, and A. D. Kline. Buffalo, N.Y.: Prometheus.

Schrag, Francis. 1989. "Values in Educational Inquiry." *American Journal of Education* 97, no. 2: 171–183.

Scriven, Michael. 1974. "The Exact Role of Value Judgments in Science." In *Introductory Readings in Philosophy of Science*. Edited by E. D. Klemke, R. Hollinger, and A. D. Kline. Buffalo, N.Y.: Prometheus, 1980.

Shipman, Marten. 1988. *The Limitations of Social Research*. 3d ed. London: Longman.

Zecha, Gerhard. 1992. "Value-Neutrality and Criticism." *Journal for General Philosophy* 23: 153–164.

Zirkle, Conway. 1959. *Evolution, Marxian Biology, and the Social Scene.* Philadelphia: University of Pennsylvania Press.

# 4

## Can, and Should, Educational Inquiry Be Scientific?

> Throughout much of its history the basic question in the philosophy of social science has been: is social science scientific, or can it be? Social scientists have historically sought to claim the mantle of science and have modeled their studies on the natural sciences. . . . However, although this approach yielded important insights into the study of human beings, it no longer grips philosophers or practitioners of social science. Some new approach more in touch with current intellectual and cultural concerns is required.
>
> Brian Fay

Near the end of chapter 3 we raised the educational form of Fay's "basic question," namely, how far can we go in studying human affairs (including educational phenomena) using the methods of natural science? In the following discussion we adopt a position nearly diametrically opposed to that of Fay quoted above (Fay 1996, 1). Postpositivists (and many practitioners of social science and educational research) hold that much educational research can be, and ought to be, "scientific." But we add the vital proviso that this position is reasonable only if the positivistic account of the nature of science prevalent in earlier times is replaced by a more up-to-date *post*positivist account. Contra Fay, this new account of the nature of science *is* in touch with what is valid in "current intellectual" concerns. (For a detailed critique of Fay's views, see Wight 1998.)

Arguments for the disjunction of natural science and social science have often rested on an unrealistic account of the nature of the natural sciences. If they are viewed according to the positivist model as based on foundationalist assumptions about evidence, proof, and truth, then social science does seem to be quite different. But when science is viewed according to the postpositivist model—in which observations are theory-laden, facts underdetermine conclusions, values affect choice of problems, and communities of researchers must examine methods and conclusions for bias—then the perceived gap between social and natural sciences begins to disappear.

Proponents of some currently popular views will not find the line of argument developed here very palatable; following Koertge and others (1998), a post-positivist is likely to regard these "contemporary cultural concerns" (especially many forms of postmodernism and social constructivism) as being "a house built on sand."

Why do some philosophers and others doubt that social and educational inquiry is (or should be or can be) scientific? Why is the naturalistic ideal for social science and related fields such as educational research (i.e., the ideal that research here can be, in vital respects, similar to research in the natural sciences) rejected? In the end, we shall argue that this rejection is mistaken, but there is undoubtedly much to learn from the points raised by the opponents of naturalistic social research.

One reason for the opposition to this ideal has already been discussed. Until a couple of decades ago the dominant account of social science was positivistic, and this rightfully was seen to be a most unpromising approach to building an effective and comprehensive account of human social phenomena. For that matter, it was also a most unpromising approach to understand even the physical and biological worlds! This is not to deny that behaviorism (in its time the most widely influential form of positivism in the social sciences and education) made a useful contribution, and it was certainly pursued with vigor. (Skinner's novel, *Walden Two*, was a brave attempt to show what an ideal society constructed on behaviorist principles could be like; see Skinner 1948.) But positivism, being an unsatisfactory philosophy of science, led to an unsatisfactory account of the roots of human action:

> We can follow the path taken by physics and biology by turning directly to the relation between behavior and the environment and neglecting supposed mediating states of mind. Physics did not advance by looking at the jubilance of a falling body, or biology by looking at the nature of vital spirits, and we do not need to discover what personalities, states of mind, feelings, traits of character, plans, purposes, intentions, or other perquisites of autonomous man really are in order to get on with a scientific analysis of behavior. (Skinner 1972, 15)

Here, in one fell swoop, Skinner has been able to get rid of much that is of interest and relevance in human life; we severely limit the scope of educational research if we abandon interest in the states of mind, feelings, plans, purposes, and intentions of students and teachers, of parents and children, of educational policy makers and curriculum developers. No wonder Fay and many others have been turned off to a "scientific approach" if this is what is understood by the phrase! But that is the wrong reaction. What we need is an account of science that does not limit the understanding of human nature so severely, and post-positivism turns out to fill this bill admirably.

Fay incorrectly states that the choice is between two alternatives—an inadequate positivistic science or an adequate nonnaturalistic approach (which he calls "perspectivism"). But in fact there are three alternatives at least: the two above, plus a third that Fay does not consider—a postpositivistic science that gives a more adequate account of the nature of the physical sciences and that applies, inter alia, to the social sciences and educational research. Karl Popper made a point similar to ours by commenting that when the critics of his position "denounce a view like mine as 'positivistic' or 'scientistic,' then I may perhaps answer that they themselves seem to accept, *implicitly and uncritically*, that positivism or scientism is *the only philosophy appropriate to the natural sciences*" (Popper 1972, 185). Like Popper, we follow the third path and adopt post-positivism as a philosophy of science adequate for understanding competent research in the natural sciences as well as in the social sciences and educational research.

Skinner's error, illustrated in the various passages from his works that we have quoted in this book, was that he started with a philosophy of science—the positivism that was prevalent when he was a student in graduate school—that he used to screen or select phenomena suitable for study. Unfortunately, the philosophy he used led him to regard unobservable entities as being unreal (or sometimes as being "prescientific" speculations; see the lengthier discussion of this in Phillips 1996)—a consequence that is as damaging to physical science as it is to psychological and educational research, for it means that subatomic particles, quantum phenomena, and black holes are as lacking in scientific merit as are the intentions, states of mind, feelings, and purposes of individuals. There is a better alternative to Skinner's procedure. The phenomena that are of interest and relevance can be selected, and then great efforts can be made to develop methods by which they can be studied rigorously and "competently." Our problems and interests can drive the development of our scientific methods, rather than vice versa.

The opponents of the naturalistic ideal in social science and educational research are apt to point out that the phenomena that are the objects of study in these fields are grossly misconceived when studied in terms of the "Cartesian-Newtonian paradigm" taken from the natural sciences. From what we have said above, it can be seen that we go some distance with them on this matter. But we do not think the answer is to abandon the naturalistic approach completely; rather, it is to grasp a more adequate account of the nature of science. To see what is at issue here, we must now turn to look at the kinds of human social phenomena that are the focus of attention in this literature and why some argue that they require a nonnaturalistic mode of explanation. (The phenomena discussed below do not exhaust the scope of social science and educational research, as some writers infer; we shall return to this issue near the end of the chapter.)

## EXPLAINING HUMAN ACTION AND HUMAN BEHAVIOR

It is common for philosophers of social science to distinguish between human *behavior* and human *action* (different individuals use different terms to label this distinction, but the terms we have chosen to use are perhaps the most common). Physical objects also exhibit behavior, but only humans can act (this latter statement might be too strong, for it could be argued that some animals can perform a limited range of actions).

A behavior is a physically (including chemically and biologically) induced and described movement or change or event: a rock can slide down a mountain in an avalanche, a comet might collide with a planet, a piece of metal will dissolve in an acid, a piece of food can be digested in an animal's stomach, a soft drink can placed in a freezer will eventually burst, a newborn baby will begin to suck. Insofar as humans are physical objects (they are made up of molecules, they occupy space, they are subject to the physical, chemical, and biological forces and processes found in nature), they also exhibit behavior. Thus, Nick falling over as a result of slipping on a banana skin is behavior, as is Denis developing a fever. Nick's arm moving up into the air is a behavior (it is a physical movement), as is Denis emitting a loud noise through his mouth. (But as we shall see, both these behaviors might also be actions.)

Philosophers give different accounts of the nature of explanation. We favor the view that to explain a behavior is to show that it was produced by some causal structure or process that exists in nature; in general this is to show that the phenomenon falls under the domain of one or more natural laws. Carl Hempel developed an earlier view that was dominant for many years, which (for expository purposes) we shall adhere to in the following (in the limit it comes close to the view we favor). The event to be explained is shown to be of the kind that the laws are applicable to, and the laws together with the specifics of the situation (the so-called initial conditions) are sufficient to account precisely for that event happening the way it did. Thus, the laws of motion, conservation of energy, and so forth, together with the details of the mass of the comet and its velocity, are sufficient to explain the behavior (the complex event) that occurs when the comet plunges into the earth. Similarly, information about Nick's muscle and bone structure, the laws of gravity, and so forth, explain what happens when he slips and falls or raises an arm. If some unexpected physical event occurs—a heavy picture falls from the wall, to use an example that recently occurred in the presence of one of the authors—then one looks to the laws that were likely to have been operating for an explanation of the picture's behavior; in this case, the weight of the picture was greater than the force of friction holding the picture hook into the soft plaster wall.

Hempel called this a "deductive nomological explanation," for it can be cast into the form of a deduction with a law (hence the "nomological") as one premise, the initial conditions as other premises, and the event or behavior that is being explained as the conclusion of the deduction. (This aspect of Hempel's theory has spawned a great deal of philosophical discussion but can serve here as the prototype of the explanation of a behavior without undue damage occurring. For a readable exposition, see Hempel 1966.) Schematically, "Why did the picture fall?" (See Figure 4.1.)

This example raises, in a very direct way, the key issue for social scientists and educational researchers: Does this pattern of explanation (or something roughly like it if Hempel's account is regarded as oversimple) work with respect to human and social phenomena? The crux of the matter (for our purposes) is whether or not there are causal structures that exist (or lawlike generalizations that apply) in these domains in the same way that they evidently do in physical nature. And this brings us to the other half of the behavior/action distinction.

Actions are things like voting, asking permission to leave the room, asking a question, shouting abuse, doing a pratfall to amuse one's grandchildren, putting down an opponent, impeaching a president, running to keep an appointment, cashing a bank check, solving an algebra problem, designing a proof for the untenability of postpositivism, going to class, cleaning the chalkboard, stopping at a red light. Actions are carried out via the medium of the physical universe—the body of a person performing an action moves, as when Nick's arm moves into the air when the chairperson of his academic department "calls the question" at a meeting or when Denis's vocal chords vibrate as he utters a loud noise (shouts) at an opponent at a meeting. (Sometimes an action is performed by a body ceasing to move, as when a pedestrian stops at a red traffic light.) But it should be apparent from these examples that the mere description of the physical events does not capture the actions *as actions*. Nick's arm moving through the air could be a nervous twitch of some kind, and more is needed to describe it as an action; Denis emitting a loud noise could be involuntary coughing, and to regard it as an action would require more into the account.

**Figure 4.1.  Explanation of Why the Picture Fell**

|  | Explanatory form | Example |
|---|---|---|
| Premise One: | Law or laws | Roughly: If the weight of an object is greater than the friction supporting it, it will fall |
| Premise Two: | Initial conditions | The picture, an object, weighed X; the force of friction was Y; X>Y |
| Conclusion: | Therefore, event to be explained | Therefore, the picture fell |

What is this extra ingredient that allows us to describe as an action what might at first appear to be solely a behavior? Several actions might involve exactly the same behavior—the person's arm moves up into the air. In one case Nick was voting by raising his arm, in another case he was seeking recognition to ask a question, and in the third case he was seeking permission to leave the room. In another type of case his arm moved into the air because of a nervous disorder that had struck him. This last case is a behavior because it was not something that Nick consciously performed—it was a movement induced physiologically and was not performed voluntarily. In the case of the three actions, what constituted the same behaviors (movement of the arm) as being different actions was the differing meanings or purposes that were being conveyed in each case (and, we might suppose, for the sake of which Nick was performing each of them).

Some philosophers have expressed this, somewhat crudely to be sure, in a type of equation: *action = behavior + meaning.* (The term "meaning" is meant to be a placeholder for some item such as the meaning, intention, reason, goal, or idea that was being expressed by the actor or the purpose that the actor hoped to achieve. A lot of ink has been spilled by philosophers debating the technical details of this account, but we hope that the general sense of the distinction has been conveyed.)

We are now in a position to discuss some important issues that arise here for the social scientist and educational researcher. Again, nothing important hangs on our choice of the particular terms "behavior" and "action"—what is important is the distinction, not the words in which it is expressed. (Colloquially we often describe actions as behaviors—even when we are not Skinnerians!—as when we praise children for "good behavior"; conversely, scientists may talk about the "action" of water in a whirlpool.)

First, it is important to note that although natural scientists might be solely interested in behaviors (in their professional role) and in the laws or theories that can explain or predict them, the social scientist and educational researcher are rarely interested in mere physico-chemical changes (or lack thereof). What is of special concern to them are the actions performed by students, parents, teachers, administrators, policy makers, and others, as well as the sociocultural contexts that provide the framework of meanings and goals and purposes and values in which these actions are located. As educational researchers, we are concerned (among other things) with what students do and don't do in classrooms, with the things that teachers do (and their reasons for so doing), the compromises that policy makers craft with each other (and what they hope to achieve by means of such compromises), and so on. The doings of students and of teachers, and the compromises reached by policy folk, all are actions, not behaviors (in the sense of the term defined above). We are also interested in the things or goals that are prized and in the values that are held—all of which are intimately related to the sociocultural settings in which the actors are located. Of course, as educational researchers we are not *solely* interested in actions; for example, we might be interested in the long-term effects of certain policies or in evaluating the effectiveness of specific educational programs and practices, or in the types of classroom organizational arrangements that are both educationally effective and cost-effective, or in the myriad factors that positively (or negatively) affect learning and motivation to learn. We shall return to these other foci of educational research at the end of the chapter. But it should be clear that human actions have a prominent place among the things that are of special concern to us because these topics—policies, programs, practices, organizations, and learning—rest on and grow out of individual and group actions.

Second, if you are performing an observational study in some educational setting, and you notice the teacher doing something that puzzles you—you can see her behavior but do not know what to make of it—the puzzle is resolved (or moves a long way toward resolution) at the same instant that you identify what the action is that the teacher is performing. Once you understand the meaning or goal or intention, *you have identified what action it is that is being performed.* (The teacher might be shouting and ranting in an apparently incoherent manner, and this puzzles you—what is happening? Then you discover that this is a unit on Roman history, and the teacher is trying to "set the class up" to understand the sense of confusion and discomfort that Romans felt when they were confronted with a mad authority figure, the emperor Caligula. Once you have identified the teacher's actions as being a "teaching illustration," the puzzle—or at least, that particular puzzle—disappears.)

Third, and crucially, there is a sense in which identifying the meaning (or purpose or intention or goal, etc.), and hence identifying the action, actually serves to *explain* it. Why is Nick's arm moving up into the air? Ah, it is because he is voting for a motion before the faculty in his department; that explains it! Of course, it does not explain why he voted for the motion—he might well have kept his arm down and only raised it when the chairperson asked, "All those against?" But that is a different question. However, even to answer why he voted the way he did—why he performed that specific action—you again need to discover his reasons or motives or purposes or values.

*What is being revealed here is a marked difference in the way in which an action and a behavior are explained.* A behavior is explained by identifying the law or theory, or the causal structures in nature, that produced the behavior; an action is explained by discovering the reasons or ideas or motives, or so forth, that constitute it to *be* an action. Once we have identified that an object of a certain mass and velocity is in a gravitational field, we have explained why it is moving the way it is; once we have discovered Nick's reasons for being in favor of the resolution that has been put forward in his faculty meeting, we have explained why he has voted for it.

The considerations, as well as the distinction, above have led some writers to argue that the study (and the explanation) of human action is nonnaturalistic; the natural science approach simply does not seem to work when human action is our focus. The argument, in outline, is this: Determining an actor's reasons or motives or so forth is an *interpretive* or *hermeneutical* activity akin to what a humanist does when he or she, say, tries to understand the actions of a character in a novel or a play (see essays in Martin and McIntyre 1994, and also those in Connolly and Keutner 1988). But before we explore this line of argument further, we offer a more detailed educational example.

## AN EXAMPLE: BENNY'S MATHEMATICS

Some years ago researcher S. H. Erlwanger (Erlwanger 1973) was out in schools studying a mathematics program called Individually Prescribed Instruction (IPI). His attention was drawn to a student identified by the teacher as perhaps slightly above average in ability whose behavior was puzzling. This young man, whom Erlwanger named "Benny," was working quietly and confidently on problems concerning fractions and decimals. Notice that even here we have departed from describing the situation strictly in terms of behavior, for we have used an interpretive process and identified that Benny was "solving problems." We have further identified these problems as involving "fractions and decimals" and thus have already started to talk in "action" terms and not strictly in "behavioral" terms. To identify ink marks on paper as being decimals, we have to understand the *meaning* of those marks, and "solving math problems" is an activity that has meaning in some cultural contexts but not in others. If we were to stick with behavior, we would simply have to say that Benny was sitting at a desk engaged in "writing behavior" or, more accurately still, engaged in "making black marks on paper"—a singularly unhelpful description of an educational situation! At any rate, what puzzled Erlwanger was that Benny often raised his hand when the teacher asked who had obtained the right answer to a problem, or he identified his answers as right when he looked them up in the textbook. Yet it was apparent to Erlwanger that Benny often had the wrong answer! Why was Benny doing this?

A person who was naively following the "physical science approach" would perhaps try to explain Benny's behavior by finding the natural law that was operating that caused Benny's hand to rise (often but not always) when the teacher emitted a certain noise. (Notice that we cannot say, within this framework, "when Benny raised his hand," for this would be a conscious action on Benny's part, and we are trying to explain his behavior; similarly, we cannot say "when the teacher asked a question," for this would be to identify the teacher's action and not the teacher's behavior.) To put it mildly, this seems to be a most unpromising route to take! Alternatively, if our researcher were a behaviorist, he or she might try to determine the "schedules of reinforcement" that Benny had been subjected to, that had conditioned him so that upon delivery of an appropriate stimulus (a verbal stimulus from the teacher) he would automatically react by having his hand raised. This seems equally unpromising as a way of explaining what was going on.

Erlwanger seems to have made the reasonable assumption that whatever Benny was doing, he was doing *on purpose*—he was acting, not merely behaving. To understand and hence to explain what Benny was doing, he started to investigate not the laws of nature that might be operating but what the boy's reasons were for claiming that his wrong answers were correct. The researcher asked Benny to explain how he was solving the math problems, and the payoff was startling! It seems that for whatever reason (perhaps he had been absent during a crucial lesson), Benny had missed out on some fundamental facts about the multiplication and division of fractions and decimals; confronted with this situation, he had attempted to make this area of mathematics meaningful to himself by inventing his own rules, ones that, as it turned out, occasionally produced the right answers. According to his own system, $2/1 + 1/2$ was equal to 1, and both $1/9$ and $4/6$ were also equal to 1. Erlwanger was able to record the entire system that Benny had constructed and thus was able to explain the answers that Benny obtained to problems. But why did Benny claim that his (often) wrong answers were right? Erlwanger asked Benny about this, and the young mathematician explained (correctly) that answers could be stated in various mathematically equivalent forms (our language, not Benny's), and he said that the textbook or the teacher was merely stating the same answer that Benny had obtained but was stating it in a different form!

In short, then, Benny's actions—his arriving at puzzling answers to math problems and his marking them as being correct—were explained by revealing the beliefs that Benny had (the various meanings and reasons he had developed that bore upon decimals and fractions). His mathematical reasoning was wrong, of course, but Benny did not realize this; he was acting according to *his* understandings, and his actions were explainable (and only explainable) in terms of these (mistaken) beliefs and reasonings. Understanding Benny's reasonings—understanding his actions rather than his bodily behaviors—was educationally productive, as it gave Erlwanger insight about what needed to be achieved to remediate the youngster's work with fractions: sadly, however, Benny's false beliefs had become so embedded by the time Erlwanger understood them that attempts to remove them were unsuccessful. The point here is that the agent's reasons and beliefs, even if they are mistaken, are typically the only way to make sense of and explain his or her actions; and knowledge of the agent's reasons is crucial if one is to plan an educational intervention. It should be clear that the level of insight we have achieved in Benny's case would not have been attained had we used, for example, a positivistic behaviorist approach—which is not to deny that using rewards and punishments, which are typical parts of the behaviorist repertoire, might be useful in working with a student like Benny. The point, however, is that in order to get the right answers consistently to the math problems, Benny's beliefs about the relevant mathematical rules had to change. Whatever methods were used to induce this, correct answers cannot be attained merely by making random marks on paper!

## SOME BACKGROUND ON HERMENEUTICS

The mode of explanation illustrated in the case of Benny, which involved interpretive or hermeneutical activity on the part of the researcher, needs further discussion. In particular we need to grapple with the issue of whether or not such explanations can be *scientific*. (In the following discussion we shall use the terms "hermeneutical" and "interpretive" and their cognates interchangeably; one term has a Greek root and the other comes from Latin, but for our purposes they can be treated as synonyms.) But first, some background will be useful.

Historically, hermeneutics developed as the science of interpreting, or ascertaining the meaning of, sacred and legal texts (hence the reference to Hermes, the messenger and interpreter of the gods). Even in the ancient world there was some recognition that laws and sacred documents were written in earlier times and for earlier audiences, and that such things as the pronouncements of the Delphic Oracle had several layers of meaning. And so the issue arose of how the meaning of these important texts was to be determined for readers and communities studying them at a later date. During the eighteenth, nineteenth, and twentieth centuries, the philosophical and methodological issues surrounding the interpretation of written texts were pursued with vigor and sophistication, and some of the conclusions reached continue to have ramifications for our own times (for a readable and brief history, see Odman and Kerdeman 1994).

To give a "gloss" on what is a much more complex story, in this latter period a theoretical move occurred that had great epistemological significance. It was argued that human voluntary action was a type of text, albeit a non-written form. Human action is laden with meaning (and meaning, of course, is a function of a sociocultural system). It is purposeful, and often it is symbolic and influenced by cultural beliefs and practices. When a researcher tries to understand what it is that a student has done, as when Erlwanger tried to identify or categorize Benny's actions, the researcher necessarily has to engage in interpretive or hermeneutical activity even when, as is perhaps usually the case, such interpretation is undertaken without specific awareness that this is what is involved (it is to be doubted that Erlwanger was consciously aware that he was engaged in a hermeneutical activity with Benny). To express this point in terms that English-language philosophers of social science prefer, an action cannot even be characterized or identified (e.g., as defiance, as an expression of illness or mental disturbance, as grandstanding, etc.) until its meaning or purpose has been ascertained.

Paul Ricoeur (Ricoeur 1977) has suggested that face-to-face oral communication and human action directly observed are easier to interpret than written texts. In the former case the "author" or "actor" is usually present in front of the interpreter and can give nonverbal cues to amplify the meaning of the verbal ones as well as provide specific correction if the interpreter seems to have made a mistake—just as Benny did when he explained to Erlwanger how he "solved" problems involving fractions. There seems to be general agreement, however, that even in the case of observed action it is far from easy to determine how an adequate interpretation can be recognized. Taking only the easiest case—that of interpreting the meaning of a single, simple gesture—considerable difficulties arise, for (as we saw earlier in the example of Nick's arm rising into the air) the fact is that all physical movements are ambiguous and could be described as constituting many different actions. (Note how parallel this is to the argument from chapter 1 that a set of data can be accommodated by more than one hypothesis.) The case of Nick's arm is in fact a form of the classic example most frequently used by philosophers, and it nicely illustrates the issues. His arm rises; but is this action the asking of a question, the seeking of permission to leave the room, voting, the greeting of a friend or the saluting of a leader, or just a muscle twitch? Even in so simple a case, interpretation is required, guided by contextual factors and so forth. How are we to go about deciding which interpretation of the arm raising is the most adequate? What, specifically, are the relevant criteria by which interpretations are to be judged? And how much guidance is it reasonable to expect from the voluminous literature on textual interpretation when what we are dealing with is the interpretation of human actions (and actions much more complex than a simple gesture)?

To the uninitiated (or even, it must be admitted, to some of the cognoscenti) the issues that arise here are mind-boggling. Are the intentions of the author or actor important or can they be ignored? Are the agent's espoused reasons always the best explanation for his or her actions? Is it sensible to suggest that there is an objective, "true" meaning or interpretation for every action? Are there as many valid interpretations as there are interpreters (as some have suggested)? Can any one individual, located as he or she is in a specific sociohistorical setting and armed with a specific set of theoretical understandings and interests, ever hope to "understand" the actions (including the spoken or written utterances) of another and almost certainly differently situated individual? (This problem is especially pertinent when the observer is from a different sociocultural group from the person observed.) Can inquiries or research projects that are at bottom interpretive in nature (and in educational research, many certainly are) meaningfully aspire to be "scientific"? Or are they more adequately thought of as humanistic endeavors? In the latter case, what features allow an interpretation to be judged as valid? Different writers give different answers to these questions; some even reject questions such as these on the grounds that they are misguided or are based on incorrect or outmoded assumptions. (See Connolly and Keutner 1988; Hiley, Bohman, and Shusterman 1991.) But now we need to turn to our own conjectures on at least some of these interrelated matters.

## INTERPRETING HUMAN ACTION AND INTERPRETING TEXTS

There are some important similarities, but also some important differences, between the constraints on educational researchers and those on scholars who interpret literature. The discussion shall proceed in a more or less orderly way, point
by point; gradually there should emerge a number of considerations bearing on
the issue of whether interpretive work can be scientific (in a nonpositivistic sense
of this term).

First, in the field of literary hermeneutics, it may well be the case that the concept of "truth" is inapplicable. Is there a truth (*one truth*) about the meaning of
Hamlet's famous soliloquy ("to be or not to be")? Is it the musing of a grief-
stricken individual or the raving of a man losing his mind? Should it be read as
indicating a certain morbidity of spirit? Does Hamlet have what we now might
call an Oedipal fixation? Do Hamlet's words merely reflect the difficulties that
individuals in Elizabethan England (including Shakespeare) had in dealing with
death? There may be many "true" ways to interpret Hamlet's soliloquy (just as
there may be false ways), just as there are many ways to "truly" read it out loud
(one of the present authors has, in his aging record collection, Sir John Gielgud,
Sir Lawrence Olivier, and John Barrymore reading the speech, with surprising
differences).

This matter has to be treated with care; at the very least, we would insist that
if there are no true and false interpretations, there certainly are better and worse
ones—just as Gielgud's and Olivier's oral interpretations of the passage arguably
are better than Barrymore's. (The complication here, of course, is that Barrymore
belongs to a now distant age, and our strong distaste may well be subjective and
simply display our own spatio-temporal location. It may indeed be a matter of
taste rather than judgment! Despite this important complication, however, strong
grounds can be presented for or against specific interpretations.)

But what about the situations commonly met by educational researchers, such
as the problem of interpreting a classroom interaction between a teacher and a
student in which (for example) the teacher appears to be severely criticizing the
student? Is "truth" also an irrelevancy here? Something *actually happened* in the
classroom, and we can give a true or false description of it. Furthermore, it might
matter a great deal that we give a true account (the teacher might be sued for
professional misconduct or fired for incompetence if we present one interpretation rather than another; or perhaps the teacher was using an experimental "push
students to their limits" approach that, if judged a success, will be recommended
to all teachers in that school district). In short, practical consequences often follow from the findings of educational research, and it behooves the researcher or
evaluator to be certain that his or her account is not fiction and is not merely "one
reading" of many that are theoretically possible concerning the situation under
investigation. It should be a good reading, a true reading. To revisit the case of
Benny, it seems clear that Erlwanger was trying to give a *true account* of what

Benny believed the rules about manipulation of fractions and decimals to be, even if the youngster's rules were not valid. Benny of course believed these rules to be true and was acting on them (recall the discussion of the issues about true and false belief in chapter 2). What would have been the point of Erlwanger giving a *false* account? He wanted to understand the real reasons for Benny's acting the way he did; he also wanted to understand properly in order to be able to help the student improve. (His account was clearly superior to one suggesting that Benny was acting arbitrarily or out of total ignorance of mathematics.)

Second, many confusions and red herrings can appear at this stage of the discussion, one of which was discussed briefly in chapter 2: those who believe (as we do) that researchers should aim to discover the truth are often accused of thinking that there is *one* ("absolute") truth.

But this is of course nonsense. Even in the literary example, several of the supposedly rival interpretations of the soliloquy actually can be true at the same time—they are not all mutually incompatible. In the classroom example involving the teacher criticizing a student, the teacher might be exercising legitimate authority, might be trying to encourage the student or set higher standards for performance, or might be expressing ethnic or sexist bias—or doing all at the same time! But whichever of these accounts of the teacher is put forward, it ought to be shown (as far as possible) to be true—for it is either true or not true that the teacher was trying to encourage the student (whether or not the actions actually achieved this) or that the teacher was ethnically biased, and so on.

Another red herring (also discussed earlier) is the argument that as the truth can never be known by mere mortals, there is no truth; as we cannot know for certain which interpretation is true, in many cases, then the notion of truth has to be abandoned. If we follow this line, we quickly arrive in the murky realm of multiple but incompatible beliefs (and even multiple incompatible realities; see Guba and Lincoln 1982; Manke 1996) about situations, all of which have to be accepted. We can do no better here than refer anyone who accepts this strange argument to philosopher John Searle's book *The Construction of Social Reality* (1995). Searle shows that the inability to decide which of several views is the correct one does not establish either that there is no correct answer or that a relativistic theory of "multiple realities" is credible. Belief in reality and in truth is not undermined by epistemological uncertainty about which account of reality is warranted.

Third, in the field of literary hermeneutics there has been a longstanding debate about the importance of authorial intent—about whether or not it is part of the interpreter's role (or a necessary part of developing an interpretation) to decipher the intent of the text's author; currently it is quite modish to hold that the purposes of the author are irrelevant (see Connolly and Keutner 1988; Fish 1980). In interpretive educational research, we suggest, the intention of the actor (the act's "author") is nearly always one important factor that needs to be considered.

Consider the two examples introduced earlier: An interpreter trying to understand the meaning of Hamlet's famous soliloquy and a researcher trying to understand the meaning of a teacher's puzzling interaction with a young student of a different ethnic background. In the literary case, it is at least coherent to argue that whatever Shakespeare had in mind is quite irrelevant; the meaning of the passage is not constituted by whatever intentions Shakespeare might have had. The words of the soliloquy are there and are "open"—we might see meanings in them that Shakespeare did not consciously intend to put there, for of course Shakespeare himself was writing under sociocultural influences of which he might not have been aware but might have influenced what he wrote—how he depicted the character of the prince of Denmark, for instance. Furthermore, we are reading the passage from our own sociotemporal location; we have several hundred more years of human history under our belts, and we have new insights into human nature available that the Bard didn't (e.g., Freudian theory which we can bring to bear upon Hamlet's musings). In light of all this, it certainly is not foolish to maintain that literary interpretation is open-ended. It might well be misguided (as was suggested in the preceding point) to seek "the true interpretation." We are free—according to this line of thought—to impose or overlay *our* meanings on the soliloquy (just as Stanley Fish famously asked his students to provide interpretations of a "poem" on the chalkboard that was actually scribbling from a previous lecture to a different class). In short, it is credible to maintain that the soliloquy has the meaning that we, individually, give it; its meaning is *imposed* or *constructed* and not *found* (see Fish 1980).

Whatever the merits of this position in the sphere of literary interpretation, it appears to be quite misguided in many educational research settings. In the example foreshadowed earlier—a teacher acting in a certain way toward a student—understanding what has transpired is not a matter of imposing our own meaning or interpretation on the situation. The problem for us researchers (assuming we are doing educational research and not gathering ideas for a novel) is, first, to comprehend what the teacher thought she was doing (after all, it was *the teacher's* action, and unless we understand *her* reasons and intentions, we do not even know what sort of action it was) and, second, to understand how the recipient, the student, interpreted the situation (for the student will react not to *our* interpretation of the situation but to *his or her own interpretation* of what the teacher was doing). In neither case are we free to impose any interpretation that we fancy, for we were not the actors involved in this situation; any account we develop as researchers has to be *strongly constrained* by the truth about those events in the classroom. Putting it in terms of the first major point made above, there is a "truth of the matter" here that (depending on the purpose of our research) it is our job to uncover if we can. The teacher meant something, and the student took it in some way or other; we can get these things right or we can get them wrong! To cling to this insight is to take the first step, not to the rigor mortis of relativism but to the rigor that is needed in a competent inquiry.

Fourth, the complexities of the sort of case we have just outlined are not always clearly teased apart by interpretivists. To make matters worse, there might be a third thing for us to do here. As researchers, we might wish to gain deeper theoretical insight into how and why situations of this type arise (e.g., why teachers of one or another ethnicity sometimes act in this way toward students of different backgrounds). It is tempting but quite misleading to describe this task as being an interpretive one. It is more accurately described as one involving theoretical explanation or analysis; having correctly interpreted the actions in the classroom, we might want to push to the level of theoretical explication. (The word "interpretation" is often used colloquially in this loose way, as when a television commentator offers an "interpretation" of some political or economic news, when what the person really is offering is a tentative hypothesis or explanation of the event in question; or perhaps it is a prognosis of what later events might unfold as a consequence of this one.) We believe it is wise to recognize that not *every* task that we undertake in research involves interpretation, and those who think that it does will be found to be using this term (or its cognate forms) in several different ways. (See Phillips 1992, chap.1, which distinguishes strong and weak senses of "interpretation.")

Fifth, we can now address the issue of whether interpretive work aimed at elucidating human actions can be scientific (in the broad sense of "scientific" accepted by postpositivists). *The most fundamental point is this*: In both the literary and educational cases discussed above, the interpreter or researcher must have some competently gathered evidence—some warrant—to back up the interpretation (or "reading of the situation") that is being given. In the case of Hamlet, the interpreter will appeal to the language of the soliloquy and perhaps to the usages and linguistic forms of the Elizabethan period. Appeal might also be made to other incidents and speeches in the play that illuminate Hamlet's character and state of mind or have significance in the light of such things as modern psychological theories that the interpreter might be disposed to use. Philosopher Dagfinn Follesdal has shown, through careful detailed analysis of a similar literary example, that the logic used in such cases is the so-called hypothetico-deductive method commonly found in the sciences (see Follesdal 1979). As we saw earlier, this is the method of forming some hypothesis, deducing its consequences, and "testing" it by looking to see if these consequences actually occur. If they do not, or if evidence that is not compatible with the hypothesis is found, then the hypothesis must be rejected as it stands.

In the education example we have been using, the researcher developing the interpretation will refer to the words (and other actions) that actually passed between the teacher and the student in the classroom but may also note the manner in which they were spoken and the body language accompanying them. But the broader context of the classroom and its makeup, and the history of the relations between teacher and student earlier in the school year, can also be sources of evidence that support the interpretation. The act of culling through this material might yield theoretical insights from various social sciences that can also be used. Finally, the educational researcher can have recourse to interviews with the teacher and the student, in which they are each asked to give an account of what happened in the classroom and what their thoughts were at the time. In collecting this evidence, the researcher will be alert for data that challenges the interpretations given by the teacher and the student and may even challenge his or her own favored view of what had happened in that particular incident.

Sixth, several points can be made that further develop the ways in which interpretive research can be expected to meet the canons of postpositivistic science:

- Both the interpreter of the soliloquy and the educational researcher are expected, by their peers and in accordance with the canons of their respective professions, to offer evidence (or warrants) to underwrite the interpretations that they put forward. Here "underwrite" means something like "indicate that the interpretation is likely to be true." An unwarranted interpretation is merely a speculation.

- It is always possible, out of the masses of material available, to select *some* items that apparently support a given interpretation, and thus the fact that the account is apparently supported by some evidence does not count for much. (As Karl Popper remarked, any fool can always find some evidence to support a favored theory.) What serves as more genuine support is that no evidence can be found to *disprove* the account that is being given; it is up to the person giving the interpretation to convince the rest of us that such negative evidence has been sought vigorously. In previous chapters we stressed that all of us have beliefs that may be based on some evidence but are nevertheless wrong. (For more discussion of the relevance of this aspect of Popper's work for educational research methodology, see Phillips 1999.)

- In both the literary and schoolroom cases, the actual interpretations that eventually are produced are themselves literary products (essays, research reports, conference papers, and so forth), but their quality *as interpretations* is judged by what they tell us about the objects or events under examination; their quality as stories or literary products is epistemically irrelevant. Thus the interpretation of the soliloquy is judged by how well it squares both with the words that Hamlet uttered and with other passages *in the play*; the account of the classroom incident is judged by the veracity of what it tells us about the words and actions *in that classroom*. Neither interpretation can be judged by qualities *purely internal to it as a literary artifact*, such as how well it is written, the seductiveness of the plot of each interpretation, and so forth. The failure to escape the internal confines of the research artifact bedevils so-called narrative research (see Phillips 1994, 1997).

- What we are getting at is found in a paper by Yvonna Lincoln with the engaging title "Emerging Criteria for Quality in Qualitative and Interpretive Research," which appeared in the journal *Qualitative Inquiry* (Lincoln 1995).

Unfortunately, by our lights Lincoln does not discuss at all the main criterion for interpretive inquiry in education; she never mentions the require-
ment that an interpretation should be borne out by the evidence—that it
should have withstood the search for negative or refuting evidence. But she
is not alone; in her paper she cites a report delivered at the annual conference of the Society for Psychotherapy Research in 1993 that gave nine guide-
lines for "judging qualitative research that is submitted for publication."
While she has a criticism to offer, she opines that "most of us would agree
that these are strong criteria or standards." In light of our previous comments,
it should be clear that one can dispute both the criteria and Lincoln's generally positive evaluation of them:

> (1) Manuscripts [must be] of archival significance. That is . . . [they must]
> contribute to the building of the discipline's body of knowledge and un-
> derstanding. (2) The manuscript specifies where the study fits within the
> relevant literature and indicates the intended contributions (purposes or
> questions) of the study. (3) The procedures used are appropriate or respon-
> sive to the intended contributions (purposes of questions posed for the
> study). (4) Procedures are specified clearly so that readers may see how
> to conduct a similar study themselves and may judge for themselves how
> well the study followed its stated procedures. (5) The research results are
> discussed in terms of their contribution to theory, content, method, and/
> or practical domains. (6) Limitations of the study are discussed. (7) The
> manuscript is written clearly, and any necessary technical terms are de-
> fined. (8) Any speculation is clearly identified as speculation. (9) The
> manuscript is acceptable to reviewers familiar with its content area and
> with its method[s]. (Elliott and colleagues, quoted by Lincoln 1995, 279)

- It might be argued that we have been a little harsh here, for surely the first
  criterion—being of "archival significance"—covers the point that is of concern to us, as does the third—the methods have to be "appropriate." But the
  passage quoted makes no mention of how this "significance" or "appropriateness" is to be determined. At the very least one might expect that somewhere in the long list of criteria *the quality of the evidence or warrants that
  are offered* could have been mentioned, together with the appropriateness
  and logical rigor of the design that was followed, the questions that were
  asked, the observations that were made, and the steps that were taken to
  eliminate rival hypotheses or interpretations. The failure to list things like
  this suggests that they play no important part in judgments of quality of
  interpretive research; certainly they cannot be assumed to be so obvious or
  so widely endorsed that they do not need to be stressed! (It is noteworthy
  that in this set of criteria the only specific point that was made about the
  procedures used in the study was that they should be clearly enough described for others to follow them if they so desired; the issue of whether the

procedures were scientifically appropriate and were likely to produce an epistemically appropriate warrant was ignored.)
- Finally, it seems to us that it behooves all interpretive researchers—whether they labor in literary or educational fields—to borrow a concept from traditional research methodology (that some would erroneously label as "positivistic"), namely, the notion of *threats to validity*. This notion originated in the fields of experimental and quasi-experimental research, in which conclusions about the effectiveness of treatments are inferred from bodies of data; however, if the experimental studies that produced these data were poorly carried out, then various threats to validity might operate that would affect the soundness of the conclusions that are reached. For example, if unmonitored and nonrandom attrition occurs from the experimental group or from the control, then the validity of the inference that the treatment produced whatever results were obtained is seriously undermined (for the "results" might be a result of the attrition, not of the treatment).

It is extremely fruitful to apply the notion of threats to validity to interpretive work. Even in literary studies, the validity of an interpretation can be undermined by such things as failure to study the language carefully or failure to consider the bearing of other parts of a text on the passage that is under present consideration. In educational field settings, the notion of threats to validity is even more important; misuse of power and the display of status by the researcher (the kinds of things that Yvonna Lincoln and others rightly are concerned about; see Lincoln 1995) can certainly undermine the quality of the data that are obtained and can thus invalidate any conclusions that are reached. But so can allowing a "mental set" to develop that biases the interpreter by blinding him or her to negative evidence (this is a well-known threat to the validity of qualitative research; see Sadler 1982); and so can the adoption of a confirmatory rather than a disconfirming mind-set (i.e., the tendency to look for positive or confirming evidence rather than evidence that disconfirms the researcher's hypothesis). Too rarely do qualitative researchers (particularly but not solely beginning researchers) think in terms of disciplining themselves to guard against these and other threats. If they were to do so, their work would indeed be more rigorous and more "competent"—and it would be "scientific" in the quite benign postpositivistic sense of the term.

Seventh, our conclusion, then, is that Skinner was wrong: *There is nothing unscientific about an educational researcher studying human actions* (not merely behaviors) and seeking to understand the reasons, beliefs, motives, purposes, and so forth, that lead individuals to act they way they do in educational and other social settings. Of course, these things can be studied in an unscientific way—when appropriate evidence is not collected, when disconfirming evidence is not sought, when hypotheses favored by the researcher are advanced without competent probing and evaluation, and when threats to the validity of the study are ignored and not countered. We researchers are human beings, and the beliefs we form are liable to be erroneous. The scientific spirit—the *postpostivistic* scientific spirit—is that, *no matter what our inquiries are about*, we should do as much as humanly possible to ensure that our beliefs are well-founded, and as Dewey said, this comes via carrying out "competent inquiries." In the words of one of Dewey's own teachers, nineteenth-century philosopher and scientist C. S. Peirce:

> A hypothesis is something which looks as if it might be true and were true, and which is capable of verification or refutation by comparison with facts. The best hypothesis, in the sense of the one most recommending itself to the inquirer, is the one which can be the most readily refuted if it is false. This far outweighs the trifling merit of being likely. For after all, what is a *likely* hypothesis? It is one which falls in with our preconceived ideas. But these may be wrong. Their errors are just what the scientific man is gunning for more particularly. (Peirce, n.d., 54)

## OTHER FOCI OF EDUCATIONAL RESEARCH

The preceding discussion focused on human voluntary actions and the mode of explanation that is appropriate for them in terms of the reasons, purposes, meanings, beliefs, and so forth, of those who are performing those actions. Undoubtedly such actions constitute an important part of what is of interest to us and affects us in our lives as members of human societies and as educationists. But we have erred if we have given the impression that actions form the *entire* subject matter of educational and social science research.

Some distinctions will prove helpful in structuring the following discussion. Virtually by definition actions have *intended consequences*, but it is crucial to note that they also have *unintended ones*; furthermore, actions are affected by a variety of *sociocultural and environmental factors*. Finally, actions can be considered *microlevel phenomena*, but there also are many *macrolevel phenomena* occurring within society. Educational research can focus on any one (or more) of these—and the way they are studied is different from the way in which it is appropriate to study actions themselves.

First, intended consequences are the ones for which the action was performed; a consequence of Denis's putting up his umbrella was that he was sheltered from the rain, and he intended this to happen; it was the very reason why he performed the action of opening the umbrella. However, as the umbrella opened it poked Nick in the eye; Denis did not intend this to happen (it was an accident), but nevertheless it was a consequence of the action, and in fact it was a more serious consequence than the one he intended! Karl Popper maintained that it is frequently the case that the unintended consequences of our actions are of more importance and significance than the intended ones; often we remain blissfully ignorant of them even after they have occurred, not realizing that they were consequences of what we have done (and we certainly did not predict that they would happen).

It is almost a platitude in the field of evaluation of educational and social programs that the side effects (i.e., the unintended consequences) of a program are often more important than the effects that the program was designed to produce. Unfortunately, it is frequently the case that the main intended effect does not materialize, but often the program still has major unintended (and unpredicted) consequences, either negative or positive. A school lunch program might not produce the consequence that was intended by the school board—significant improvement in the level of nourishment of students—but it might serve as a jobs program for members of the community and thus indirectly affect the well-being of some students in ways that the members of the board neither realized nor intended. (Unintended consequences can be either positive or negative, of course. A needy student's parent obtaining a part-time job related to the lunch program is probably positive; the lowered performance of some students after the lunch period, if it occurred, would be negative.) This illustrates the fact that documenting and precisely measuring the consequences of educational policies and actions can be an important aspect of educational research (often with major policy implications), and this might not involve the researcher in hermeneutical work at all (or at least, not the degree of it that is involved in trying to understand the actions of an individual or a committee or a policy-setting board). What it requires is a method of observing consequences and tracing lines of causation back to policies or choices that may not have had these consequences as an aim (see, e.g., the voluminous research on the "hidden curriculum" of schools).

To use another example, documenting the effects of introducing an educational voucher scheme into a state might be an important research activity and might involve determining the types of schools to which families of different socioeconomic status (SES) or ethnicity send their children; this research might even produce generalizations that are rather similar in form to those found in the natural sciences (perhaps something like "the probability of a child from socioeconomic background X remaining in a public school until graduation is Y"). This sort of research is different from research aiming to understand the reasons for a particular family with socioeconomic background X deciding to leave their child in a public school. The latter is unambiguously a project involving interpretive methods whereas the former is not.

Second, the actions of educators and the enactment by individuals of educational policies and practices take place in specific sociocultural settings that affect both the actions and their consequences. Even the physical environment can affect actions and their consequences (a teacher's action that might pass almost unnoticed by the pupils in cool weather might provoke a riot when the classroom is unbearably hot and humid, and the way the teacher actually acts might be shaped by the temperature or other conditions in the classroom). Once again these things can be the focus of the researcher's attention, and in many cases interpretive methods will not be appropriate to use. Consider another case: A researcher might be studying the mathematics education of girls in Japan as compared with those in the United States. The educational practices with respect to math will probably be influenced by the differing roles of women in these societies, by the economic opportunities available, by family and societal values, and so forth. Studying these factors, and how they influence the treatment that girls receive, is not necessarily a hermeneutical activity, although aspects of the research could be framed so that they are hermeneutical.

Third, in some respects individuals and their actions can be regarded as the microlevel in society, just as for some purposes atoms or perhaps quarks can be regarded as constituting the microlevel in physical nature. Although at the microlevel in society we have individuals *acting,* it is important to note that not all microlevel phenomena involving individuals require that we seek their reasons, motives, or beliefs for acting. For example, we could collect test scores (without worrying about the reasons why students answered the tests the way they did) and analyze them, or we could tally which individuals dropped out of high school and relate this to their SES levels or ethnic backgrounds or IQ scores (again without being concerned to discover the reasons that the individuals concerned gave for dropping out).

It will hardly come as a surprise that in addition to the microlevel, there is a "macrolevel" as well or, more accurately, there are several such levels. Thus, in the physical universe there are atoms that are made up of quarks, molecules that are made up of atoms, complex compounds that are composed of different types of molecules, biological organisms that are made up of complex compounds, and ecosystems that are made up of various biological organisms. There are also artifacts or effects produced by organisms or physical objects (landslides, beehives, nests, dung, the destruction of forests or grasslands). Similarly, in the human sphere there are individuals, groups made up of individuals, and complex societies made up of groups, but there also are organizations (the Senate, the Marine Corps, the Ford Motor Company, the local school board), humanly produced artifacts (bridges, freeway systems, schoolrooms), and of course such things as customs, laws, and norms. Of particular interest, as we shall see below, are the macrophenomena that are in some sense the resultants or "sums" of the actions of individuals.

The methods appropriate for investigating phenomena at one level in nature might not be appropriate for working at other levels. The conceptual apparatus might need to be different at each level, and the laws and theories applicable at one might not be applicable at another. Thus, in the physical universe, the subatomic realm is marked by randomness and unpredictability, yet at the macrolevels there are the substantial regularities we call the "laws of nature." In a sense, these macroregularities result in some way from the randomness at the lowest microlevel. The methods, concepts, and theories used by organic chemists, population geneticists or ecologists are not the same as those used by particle physicists or cosmologists. Paralleling all this, we can think of lawlike regularities that occur in the human realm as a result of the random voluntary actions of large numbers of individuals at the microlevel, and different methods are required for the study of these different phenomena. For example, at the microlevel Nick and Denis and their spouses and friends spend their income in the ways they individually see fit, and these ways may be quite different. Yet at the macro or societal level the disparate spending patterns of individuals may be describable in terms of regularities that are codified in the so-called laws of economics (and the methods appropriate for studying these micro and macro phenomena are quite different). Discovering these macrolevel regularities and the factors that influence them is an important facet of social science and educational research, and it can look remarkably like research in the natural sciences.

Many economists, macrosociologists, organizational theorists, political scientists, and comparative educationists are professionally concerned with the happenings and regularities at the macrolevel in society and also across societies (such things as dropout rates and their relationships with ethnicity or SES; the difference in economic and educational attainment between "voluntary" and "involuntary" migrant groups to a country like the United States; entry rates of women into the science-related professions; societal and economic factors that influence the introduction of compulsory education laws in third world countries). We must not forget, either, the work of many psychologists who focus on aspects of learning, motivation, memory, and so forth, that all humans have in common; much work in psychology is reminiscent of research in areas of biology—one thinks of Piaget and his influential stage theory of cognitive development that he believed applied to all humans in all cultures. *There is no reason in principle why such macrolevel educational research cannot be naturalistic*, and this is why there is an important place in the training of educational researchers for instruction in descriptive and inferential statistics, sampling theory, experimental and quasi-experimental design, mathematical modeling, the use of observational techniques, the rigorous analysis of qualitative data, the construction of tests and measures, and the rest.

Part of the postpositivist view of research, as we have presented it here, is a certain pluralism of method. It is not the particular *type* of research that makes it scientific, on this view. One can study individuals or groups; one can study personal actions or patterns that appear at a higher level of social aggregation or organization; one can study intentions or unintended consequences; one can pursue experimental, interview, observational, statistically oriented, or interpretive research—or some combination of these (even if some will say these can't be combined). The postpositivist approach to research is based on seeking appropriate and adequate *warrants* for conclusions, on hewing to standards of truth and falsity that subject hypotheses (of whatever type) to test and thus potential disconfirmation, and on being open-minded about criticism.

## AN EXAMPLE OF NONINTERPRETIVE RESEARCH INVOLVING MICROLEVELS AND MACROLEVELS

In 1997, Valerie Lee and Julia Smith published the paper "High-School Size: Which Works Best and for Whom?" (Lee and Smith 1997). They built upon earlier theoretical and empirical work, much of it coming from the "school restructuring" literature, which suggested that students learn more in small high schools and that learning was more equitable in these settings (in the sense that the gap in performance between white and higher SES students, on one hand, and minority and lower SES students, on the other, was narrower in such schools). But the amount of evidence was not great, and there was the unresolved issue of just how small a school had to be to maximize this effect; there also were issues about the precise size of this effect for various social groups.

Lee and Smith made use of a national data set known as NELS:88 ("National Education Longitudinal Study 1988"); these data had been collected on a large number of students across the United States, and these had been collected from the same students when they were in eighth, tenth, and twelfth grades. (The data included information about the schools of the students, their SES and ethnic backgrounds, and their scores on "objective tests" in various subjects including mathematics and reading, the two areas on which the researchers chose to focus.)

The investigators took data from NELS about students who stayed at the same high school until graduation, about whom there was sufficient data to validate the proposed analytic methods. Their sample contained 9,812 students from 789 public, Catholic, and elite private high schools. They then made a number of sophisticated statistical adjustments to deal with certain problems, such as the fact that certain categories of schools and students were "oversampled" by the procedure outlined above, and therefore their initial sample was unrepresentative of the population as a whole. Of course they had to analyze students' test scores to "capture students' pattern of performance in terms of number correct on an estimated continuum of items scaled by difficulty level and equated across grades and forms [of the tests]" (Lee and Smith 1997, 209). (Difficulty level is not determined by asking students about their beliefs or judgments, for researchers regard this as too "subjective"; rather, "difficulty" is defined "objectively" in terms of percentages of students who get an item wrong. We have put "scare quotes" around several terms here that some would want to question, but clearly there is something to be said for this widespread research practice, and indeed it has proven to be fruitful.)

Another important methodological aspect of the study was developed in response to the fact that high school enrollments vary. They do not come conveniently divided by nature into groups containing the same number of students but technically constitute what is known as a "continuous variable." Thus the researchers had to decide on what categories to form, and they settled on "schools with 300 students or less," "301–600," "601–900," "901–1,200," "1,201–1,500," "1,501–1,800," "1,801–2,100," and "over 2,100." Finally, Lee and Smith used a technique of statistical analysis known as hierarchical linear modeling (HLM), and their findings were presented in tables and graphs, with accompanying discussions. (Obviously, we cannot reproduce all of them here, but their data, and their analyses, are reported quite fully for the inspection of their scientific peers. As well as the tables and graphs reporting the results, there are almost four and a half pages of technical appendices). They summarized their findings in the abstract to their article:

> Results suggest that the ideal high school, defined in terms of effectiveness (i.e., learning), enrolls between 600 and 900 students. In schools smaller than this, students learn less; those in large high schools (especially over 2,100) learn considerably less. Learning is more equitable in very small schools, with equity defined by the relationship between learning and student socioeconomic status (SES). (Lee and Smith 1997, 205)

Lee and Smith were evidently not trying to understand the *actions* of individual students using hermeneutical methods; rather, they were studying the difference in test scores across a particular category of social institution (i.e., schools), the members of which varied in size. We may say that the study as a whole focused on the relation between macrolevel and microlevel phenomena (between school size and individual performance on tests in certain subjects) and was naturalistic through and through. Compare it with a study in which, say, an agricultural scientist examines the milk production from different types of cows that are feeding in fields having different herd densities. Unflattering as it may seem, there appears to be no significant difference in general logic between the two studies! It is also evident, however, that Lee and Smith documented something that has great relevance for policy: If we are about to construct new schools, we ought to give some thought to limiting their size.

But what are we to make of the suggestion that school size is a *causal factor*? How can size of the school population cause increased or decreased learning to take place in individuals? Lee and Smith are quite clear about this, and relatively sophisticated:

> We suggest that the effects [of size] on learning are probably indirect, mediated by their influence on basic features of the academic and social organization and functioning of schools (variables that were not in our models). Under this explanation,

size serves as a facilitating or inhibiting factor for fundamental educational processes in schools. (Lee and Smith 1997, 219)

In other words, Lee and Smith were acknowledging indirectly that learning is an *action* of students. Their study throws light on an important factor that can influence individuals, but their study does not rule out the possibility that other studies would be fruitful. We can imagine that useful studies could be performed using other methods, such as "shadowing" or interviewing students in different-sized schools, studying the interactions among students in large and small schools, or cataloguing the different range of educational opportunities that exist in schools of different sizes. All these studies would complement each other—they would not be rivals. *This underscores the moral that there is no one favored type of study for the postpositivist—what type of study is best depends on the problem or issue that is under investigation; on important matters it is possible that studies of different types can make a contribution.* What is crucial is that, whatever methodological approach is adopted, the study be rigorous, or as Dewey would say, "competent."

## A NOTE ON CAUSATION IN THE SOCIAL WORLD

Lee and Smith are to be admired for having realized that their work raised an issue about causation: Can school size be a causal factor influencing something like student achievement? Scholars who see society only as a site for human action and disregard or do not see anything else of importance are likely to believe that it is a serious mistake to adopt a naturalistic view of causation in the social sciences. Their model is much closer to the notion of causation that is to be found in many (but not all) works of literature. Some of the events in the last part of Sean O'Casey's famous play *Juno and the Paycock* can serve as a typical example. When the daughter is discovered to be pregnant, her father interprets her pregnancy as an affront to his standing in the community and threatens to throw her out of the house (his reaction is shaped, to some degree, by the fact that this is the only one of his several misfortunes that he can do anything about). His wife says that if he makes good on his threat, she also will leave; he then decides to go to the pub to have a drink with "the few friends he has left." Here the actions of each individual are interpreted by the others and thus have meaning for them. Each individual then reacts to these perceived meanings by performing actions that in turn are interpreted—and then reacted to—by the other characters. To use a famous expression coined by anthropologist Clifford Geertz, the characters are caught up in webs of meaning that they themselves have constructed—a phenomenon that looks quite unlike the operation of causal chains in the physical domain.

Despite the attractiveness of this analysis, we insist that there are many causal chains operating in the social realm, at both the microlevel and the macrolevel, which can be studied naturalistically. Indeed, a regular causal analysis is not completely out of reach even with the sorts of events depicted in the play, events that clearly involved the actions of individuals at the microlevel. There are several points to be made here.

First, in a straightforward sense, we can say that the father's actions helped cause the reactions of the other characters, who were part of the causal nexus that was operating. If he had acted differently, a different set of reactions probably would have ensued. Fathers, no less than anyone else, constantly shape the actions of others—and often do it quite deliberately. All of us influence others and find them understandable and predictable, because in general their beliefs and desires and interpretations of their situations are causally related to the ways they act; we influence their actions by changing or "manipulating" these things. This is not to say that if a father act in manner A, his daughter will *necessarily* act in the manner B that he had predicted. But even if she doesn't act this way, his doing A still was part of the reason she did what she did do (it was part of the causal nexus, and possibly it played a necessary part in leading to what she did do).

Second, in the paragraph above we used language that was chock-full of references to causation; sometimes this was thinly disguised, but it was causal nonetheless. An action is *likely to lead*, we constantly *shape*, and we *influence*—all these are causal expressions. Family therapists intervene and try to change the ways family members act, for they realize (perhaps only partly consciously) that such changes will produce other changes (*will produce* is another causal expression). Social life would become impossible if causation of some sort did not exist. Mario Bunge put the point nicely:

> Rational action and the rational discussion of it are among the features that distinguish society from nature, and consequently social science from natural science. However, this distinction should not be overdone, *for reason is impotent without causation.* (Bunge 1996, 36; emphasis added)

Third, the methods of scientific inquiry—interpreted in the broad postpositivistic manner outlined in this book—are as useful (and as necessary) at the microlevel of human action as they are in studying causal mechanisms at the macrolevel in society and in biological and physical nature. There is no doubt, as the discussion in this chapter should have convinced you, that the *nature* of the causal influences or mechanisms differs in these various domains. But, if we believe there are causal mechanisms of whatever type operating (fully deterministic, probabilistic, depending on the operation of natural laws, or depending on the existence of webs of meanings and sociocultural values, etc.), then we need to produce "competent" warrants to back up the claims that we are making. But we are not free to believe anything we please about the factors that are operating in any given situation.

Here again, an overly rigid deterministic conception of causation promulgated in the positivistic account of science has encouraged the view that causation cannot obtain in the social and human realms. As we have tried to show, however, causation can take many forms, and it is necessary on almost any account of connectedness and influence in the human realm. (Whenever one says "this happened because of that," some type of causal link is being assumed, even if it is not a lawlike, deterministic type of link.)

It might be thought that researchers working in the macrodomain or in the biological or natural sciences are fortunate because they have the option of performing controlled experiments (these being the strongest designs for establishing that causal links exist). But anthropologists and others doing qualitative studies of human groups have found that they can test their hypotheses about the human dynamics that are at work in various ways, for example, by intervening and asking a key person in the group to act in a somewhat different way so that it can be seen if this will produce a different outcome. (In classroom research, teachers in different classrooms are sometimes given different "scripts" to follow for the same reason.) Generally, observing that event or action A is "correlated" with some outcome B, or is followed by B, is not a strong enough warrant for believing that A is part of the cause of B. Neither is it a valid warrant to cite your own feeling of certainty that A resulted in B, or to claim that it is impossible in your view for A not to have done so. Feelings, no matter how strongly held, are only feelings. As Mario Bunge is quoted in the epigraph to chapter 3, "we often mistake opinions for data, value judgments for descriptive statements, and prophecies for forecasts."

So much for thoughts inspired by *Juno and the Paycock*. We need to remind you that at the microlevel there are other causal phenomena besides the ones we have been discussing. As we pointed out earlier in this chapter, human actions have unintended consequences, often precipitating unintended causal chains that operate out of our control (and often without our knowledge). Denis consumes a banana and carelessly tosses the skin over his shoulder; the skin is a causal factor in Nick's slipping; in doing so he knocks over an elderly lady, who . . . Or consider a more uplifting example: When Denis was a high school teacher, he strongly praised the prose style of a young student who had written an essay for his class (a deliberate action on his part, no doubt, even if he could not foresee all of its consequences); this praise motivated the student to continue with her writing, unleashing an unintended but nevertheless highly desirable train of events that culminated in her winning the Nobel Prize for literature many decades later. Would we not want to say that Denis's action was, if not *the* cause, then certainly *part* of the causal chain that led to this award? After all, if he had not acted in this way at a crucial stage in the student's life, then a different chain of events might have been unleashed. Of course the chain of events starting with his act of praise might have turned out differently anyway—chains of events involving humans do not run quite like clockwork, a theme of many Hollywood movies! (Thornton Wilder's famous novel *The Bridge at San Luis Rey* and Robert Altman's film *Nashville* depict the unlikely chains of events that led certain people to be present at the one place at the one time when a disaster occurred; if one thing had happened differently, a different group might have assembled.)

If you hesitate to give Denis credit for his student's achievement, are you then denying that teachers have a causal influence on students' learning? And if you deny this, why do you advocate that we educate children? If we have no impact, isn't it a waste of time? And why do the faculty members in teacher-training programs put so much effort into getting student-teachers to act in certain ways if they do not regard these ways of acting as being efficacious (another causal term) in producing learning in schoolchildren?

One point of our discussion has been that, at the microlevel, causal language (whether or not it involves the actual term "cause") is hardly avoidable; the same can be said for the macrolevel. Increasing family stability and family income are not only correlated with increased student learning; they are probably causal factors in producing this effect. Working in cooperative groups causes an increase in some types of learning and in various motivational outcomes; having clear classroom rules and expectations is causally related to student learning. Again, without causal mechanisms and attendant regularities, there could be no educational planning, no educational reform, and indeed no social life. (Without causal mechanisms our actions would not even have unintended consequences, for these were *caused* by our actions even though we did not intend them or expect them to occur.)

To sum up, then, the issue is not whether we should seek to study and understand causal relationships; it is how we are to uncover them and use them to best advantage in promoting the improvement of education. In principle the answer is simple: Whether at the microlevel of human actions and their consequences or at the macrolevel in society, the techniques of competent naturalistic inquiry are called for. We need to recognize that each and every one of us is apt to believe that we have sophisticated insight into how the society of which we are members operates, and it behooves us to recall the quotation from Oliver Cromwell in the opening pages of this book—we should bethink that we might be mistaken! We also are apt to be seduced by correlations, and by apparent regularities, into thinking that we have grasped the relevant causal structures. Similarly, we are prone to ignore—to overlook or not to see—phenomena that indicate that our "understandings" are misunderstandings (negative evidence is usually more difficult for us to take note of than the positive). We need disciplined, competent inquiry to establish which of our beliefs are warranted and which are chimerical. And the philosophy that will serve us best in our endeavors is *postpositivism*.

## FINAL WORDS: THE UNITY OF SCIENCE?

We opened this book with the thought that in the contemporary world scientists have fallen from the pedestals they occupied in Auden's day—they are no longer thought of as "dukes." Yet at the end of our journey we seem to have reinstated some measure of respect for them, for we have given the impression that scientific inquiry (in its postpositivist guise) can be used productively everywhere— in the study of physical and biological nature, in the study of macrophenomena in society, and in the study of human actions and other microphenomena. We even embraced "competent inquiry" in hermeneutics and in literary interpretation. All this, in effect, leaves precious few domains where scientific inquiry cannot be used. What hubris!

But, even worse, we can be charged with having surreptitiously reinstated one important doctrine of positivism (and particularly of logical positivism)—the doctrine of "unified science." The logical positivists hoped for a unification of all branches of science, chiefly by way of a unified observation language that would cut across all domains (it will be recalled from our discussion in chapter 1 that observation and the realm of observable phenomena were central to the logical positivists). Other philosophers and scientists have expected that all branches of science will eventually be unified by being "reduced" to some basic theory or set of theories (usually thought to be theories of physics, such as the well-known but as yet undiscovered physical "theory of everything"). For example, psychology (on this view) will eventually be reduced to biology (in the sense that psychological phenomena, and psychological theories, will be derivable in some way from the laws and theories of biology), and biology will be reducible (in the same sense) to chemistry, and chemistry to physics, and the laws of physics will be reducible to (i.e., derivable from) this "theory of everything," which would be the basic and foundational theory! Clearly some aspects of this program have been carried out; some (but by no means all) aspects of biology have been reduced to chemistry, much of chemistry has been reduced to physics, and currently there is a popular line of research attempting to relate psychology more closely to biology and brain physiology. Whether the whole program is more than a pipe dream is a matter of great controversy; see, for example, the discussion of this in John Dupre's *The Disorder of Things* (1993).

We have not taken a stand on these varieties of "unified science." Rather, the position we have been developing in this book is closer in spirit to the views of two very strong antipositivists—John Dewey and Karl Popper—two philosophers who held different views on many topics (although there are surprising overlaps in some aspects of their thought; see Phillips 1992, chap.6). One thing that unites these men is the view that "competent inquiry" has rather similar features in whatever field it takes place. In his book *How We Think*, Dewey preferred to call this "reflective thinking" rather than "scientific thinking," but the book makes his meaning clear (part of his point in avoiding the latter expression was his view that this type of thinking is found in *all* cases of effective inquiry and not just in the fields traditionally regarded as science). Because he used the same example we used in an earlier chapter—the case of Columbus and his challenge to the prevailing view that the earth was flat—it is appropriate to quote him at some length:

> The earlier thought, belief in the flatness of the earth, had some foundation in evidence; it rested upon what men could see easily within the limits of their vision. But this evidence was not further looked into; it was not checked by considering other evidence; there was no search for new evidence. Ultimately the belief rested on laziness, inertia, custom, absence of courage and energy in investigation. The later belief [i.e., that held by Columbus] rests upon careful and extensive study, upon purposeful widening of the area of observation, upon reasoning out the conclusions of alternative conceptions to see what would follow in case one or the other were adopted for belief. . . . because Columbus did not accept unhesitatingly the current traditional theory, because he doubted and inquired, he arrived at his thought. . . . he went on thinking until he could produce evidence for both his confidence and his disbelief. . . . *Active, persistent, and careful consideration of any belief or supposed form of knowledge in the light of the grounds that support it and the further conclusions to which it tends* constitutes reflective thought. (Dewey 1971, 8–9; his emphasis)

Postpositivism of this type, in our view, *is* broadly applicable to all inquiries that aim to be competent, and in this sense there is a unity across domains—a unity of effective and disciplined inquiry. As Dewey put it later in his *Logic: The Theory of Inquiry*, "the different objectives of common sense and of scientific inquiries demand different subject-matters," but "this difference in subject-matters is not incompatible with the existence of a common pattern" (Dewey 1966, 116).

## REFERENCES

Bunge, Mario. 1996. *Finding Philosophy in Social Science*. New Haven: Yale University Press.

Connolly, J., and T. Keutner, eds. 1988. *Hermeneutics Versus Science*. Notre Dame, Ind.: University of Notre Dame Press.

Dewey, John. [1933] 1971. *How We Think*. Chicago: Henry Regnery/Gateway.

Dewey, John. [1938] 1966. *Logic: The Theory of Inquiry*. New York: Henry Holt.

Dupre, John. 1993. *The Disorder of Things*. Cambridge: Harvard University Press.

Erlwanger, S. 1973. "Benny's Conception of Rules and Answers in IPI Mathematics." *Journal of Children's Mathematical Behavior* 1, no. 2: 7–26.

Fay, B. 1996. *Contemporary Philosophy of Social Science*. Oxford: Blackwell.

Fish, S. 1980. *Is There a Text in This Class?* Harvard: Harvard University Press.

Follesdal, D. 1979. "Hermeneutics and the Hypothetico-Deductive Method." *Dialectica* 33: 319–336.

Guba, E., and Y. Lincoln. 1982. *Effective Evaluation*. San Francisco: Jossey-Bass.

Hempel, C. 1966. *Philosophy of Natural Science*. Englewood Cliffs, N.J.: Prentice-Hall.

Hiley, D., J. Bohman, and S. Shusterman, eds. 1991. *The Interpretive Turn*. Ithaca, N.Y.: Cornell University Press.

Koertge, N., ed. 1998. *A House Built on Sand*. New York: Oxford University Press.

Lee, V., and J. Smit. 1997. "High School Size: Which Works Best and for Whom?" *Educational Evaluation and Policy Analysis* 19. no. 3: 205–227.

Lincoln, Y. 1995. "Emerging Criteria for Quality." *Qualitative Inquiry* 1, no. 3: 275–289.

Manke, M. 1996. "Seeking Ammunition for the Epistemological Wars." *Educational Foundations* 10, no. 1: 73–80.

Martin, M., and L. McIntyre. 1994. *Readings in the Philosophy of Social Science*. Cambridge: Bradford Books/MIT Press.

Odman, P.-J., and D. Kerdeman. 1994. "Hermeneutics." In *International Encyclopedia of Education*. Edited by T. Husen and N. Postlethwaite. 2d ed. Oxford: Pergamon.

Peirce, C. n.d. *Philosophical Writings of Peirce*. Edited by Justus Buchler. New York: Dover.

Phillips, D. C. 1992. *The Social Scientist's Bestiary*. Oxford: Pergamon.

Phillips, D. C. 1994. "Telling It Straight: Issues in Assessing Narrative Research." *Educational Psychologist* 29, no. 1: 13–21.

Phillips, D. C. 1996. "Philosophical Perspectives." In *Handbook of Educational Psychology*. Edited by D. Berliner and R. Calfee. New York: Macmillan.

Phillips, D. C. 1997. "Telling the Truth about Stories." *Teaching and Teacher Education* 13, no. 1: 101–109.

Phillips, D. C. 1999. "How to Play the Game: A Popperian Approach to the Conduct of Educational Research." In *Critical Rationalism in Educational Discourse*. Edited by G. Zecha. Amsterdam: Rodopi.

Popper, K. 1972. *Objective Knowledge*. Oxford: Clarendon.

Ricoeur, P. 1977. "The Model of the Text." In *Understanding and Social Inquiry*. Edited by F. Dallmayr and T. McCarthy. Notre Dame, Ind.: Notre Dame University Press.

Sadler, D. 1982. "Intuitive Data Processing as a Potential Source of Bias in Naturalistic Evaluations." *Evaluation Studies Review Annual*, Vol 7. Edited by E. House et al. Books on Demand.

Searle, J. 1995. *The Construction of Social Reality*. New York: Free Press.

Skinner, B. F. 1948. *Walden Two*. New York: Macmillan.

Skinner, B. F. 1972. *Beyond Freedom and Dignity*. London: Jonathan Cape.

Wight, C. 1998. "Philosophical Geographies: Navigating Philosophy in Social Science." *Philosophy of the Social Sciences* 28, no. 4: 552–566.

# Index

action: versus behavior, 68–70; definition of, 69; interpretation of, 76–83; scientific accounts of, 68–74
Allen, Woody, 32, 49
Auden, W. H., 1, 4, 93
auxiliary assumptions, 19–22
Ayer, A. J., 9

Barry, Marion, 41
Bayes, Thomas, 24
behavior: versus action, 68–70; definition of, 68; scientific accounts of, 68–72; Skinner on, 9–10
beliefs: acceptance of, 39–40; definition of, 36; false, 2–3, 6; multiple, 35–40, 77; necessity of, 32–35; versus truth, 2–4, 40
*The Bell Curve* (Herrnstein & Murray), 58–59
Benny, 72–74
bias, 40–43; definition of, 41; detection of, 59–61; external influence and, 53; versus perspective, 46–47
Binet, Alfred, 56–57
Bridgman, Percy, 10
Broca, Paul, 48
Bunge, Mario, 45, 90–91
Burt, Cyril, 55, 58

Campbell, Donald, 13
causation: versus correlation, 88–89; in social world, 89–92

cognitive values. *See* internal values
Collins, Harry, 33
community, epistemic, feminism on, 60–61
competent inquiries, 4, 43, 83, 89; and objectivity, 45–46
Comte, Auguste, 8–9
consequences, 75; of educational policy, 84; intended versus unintended, 83–84
consequent, affirming, 21
constructivism, social. *See* social constructivism
correlation, versus causation, 88–89
Cromwell, Oliver, 2–3, 92

Darwin, Charles, 56
Descartes, Rene, 6, 15
Dewey, John, 3–4, 31, 36, 38, 83, 93–94
Duhem-Quine thesis, 19–22
Dupre, John, 93

Edinburgh school, 33
educational research: noninterpretative, 87–89; scientific method and, 65–95; topics in, 2, 83–87
Eisner, Elliot, 38
Elgin, Catherine, 29, 31
empiricism, 5–7; and positivism, 7–11
environmental factors, and actions, 83–85
epistemically relevant values, 52–55
epistemic community, feminism on, 60–61

97

# About the Authors

D. C. Phillips was born and educated in Australia, and moved to the United States in 1974; currently he is professor of education, and by courtesy, professor of philosophy at Stanford University (where he is also the Associate Dean for Academic Affairs in the School of Education). He was president of the Philosophy of Education Society during its golden jubilee year in 1990–1991; in 1993 he was Christensen Fellow at St. Catherine's College, Oxford; and he is a Fellow of the International Academy of Education. He has authored, coauthored, or edited ten books and written more than a hundred journal articles and book chapters, which span educational research and evaluation methodology, philosophy of social science, philosophy of education, and history of nineteenth- and twentieth-century thought. He has given workshops on issues related to the present volume in the United States, Australia, Israel, New Zealand, Norway, Sweden, and Switzerland.

Nicholas C. Burbules is professor of educational policy studies at the University of Illinois, Urbana/Champaign. He has published numerous articles and several books in the areas of philosophy of education and educational policy. His recent books include *Watch IT: The Promises and Risks of New Information Technologies for Education* (Boulder, Colorado: Westview Press, forthcoming), written with Thomas A. Callister, Jr., and *Globalization and Education: Critical Perspectives* (New York: Routledge, forthcoming), co-edited with Carlos Torres. Currently he serves as editor of the journal *Educational Theory*.